Spirituality
YOU CAN live WITH

— stronger faith in 30 days —

CHRIS PADGETT

PUBLISHED BY ST. ANTHONY MESSENGER PRESS
CINCINNATI, OHIO

Cover design by LUCAS Art & Design, Jenison, Michigan
Cover image © Masterfile
Book design by Mark Sullivan

LIBRARY OF CONGRESS CATALOGING-IN-PUBLICATION DATA
Padgett, Chris, 1970-
A spirituality you can live with : stronger faith in thirty days / Chris Padgett.
p. cm.
Includes bibliographical references and index.
ISBN 978-0-86716-968-3 (pbk. : alk. paper) 1. Spirituality—Catholic Church. I. Title.
BX2350.65.P34 2011
248.4'82—dc22
2010047957

ISBN 978-0-86716-968-3

Published by Servant Books, an imprint of St. Anthony Messenger Press.
28 W. Liberty St.
Cincinnati, OH 45202
www.AmericanCatholic.org
www.ServantBooks.org

Printed in the United States of America.

Printed on acid-free paper.

11 12 13 14 15 5 4 3 2 1

Thanks to my family, especially Linda.

INTRODUCTION

How to Use This Book | *vii*

CHAPTERS:

1 : *There Must Be More to Life* | *1*

2 : *It's All About Relationship* | *5*

3 : *Brokenness: The Upside to the Downside* | *8*

4 : *Weakness Needs a Helping Hand* | *12*

5 : *Emptied to Be Filled* | *15*

6 : *God's Love Poured Out: The Trinitarian Perspective* | *19*

7 : *Who Are You?* | *22*

8 : *Where Are You?* | *26*

9 : *Who Is Your Neighbor?* | *31*

10 : *Living Your Love* | *35*

11 : *God Chooses* You! | *40*

12 : *Finding Solitude in the Chaos* | *46*

13 : *When the Feeling's Gone: Dryness and Distraction* | *52*

14 : *Sin and Spirituality* | *58*

15 : *Virtuous Reality* | *64*

16 : *Warning: Spiritual Elitism* | *68*

17 : *A Spiritual Buffet* | *71*

18 : *Sacraments and Sacramentals* | *75*

19 : *Our Spirituality Is Biblical* | *79*

20 : *Mary's Place* | *83*

21 : *Forgiveness Is Essential* | *89*

22 : *Love Means Sacrifice, Service, Mediation, and Advocacy* | *92*

23 : *From the Heart* | *99*

24 : *Willing the Good in the Moment* | *102*

25 : *Spirituality of the Senses* | *109*

26 : *Snake Kissing and Other Extremes* | *113*

27: *Taxicab Spirituality* | *117*

28 : *Facts About Fasting* | *120*

29 : *Saintly Examples* | *122*

30 : *A Spiritual Pep Talk* | *139*

NOTES | *132*

How to Use This Book

We could all use a spiritual retreat now and then, but for many of us, our lives are too busy. The demands of daily life prevent us from finding quality time to advance our spiritual life. What can we do? Allow me to explain how this book could assist you in a little retreat.

St. Ignatius provided amazing insights into the reality of authentic spirituality. He realized that there were times in our life when feelings could be very influential in how we act, for the good or for the bad. He introduced some very important guidelines, derived from his life experiences, concerning these times of "consolation" and "desolation" in which we all partake. The result was a set of spiritual practices, or "exercises," through which, over a specific amount of time, people could enter into deeper intimacy with God.

In some ways this little offering of mine is an attempt to extend insight into a spirituality that I am still unfolding and applying in my own life. These reflections are not simply ideological; rather, they're experiential.

Our spiritual life has to be something we can actually live rather than just dream, discuss, or study in a book. In these pages are a few ways I have found that I can actually "do" spirituality.

These insights have worked for others too, which is why I want to share them with you.

Questions of our brokenness and the inability to implement structure into our lives often accompany discussions concerning spiritual practices. We also need to look at our vocation in life and how that impacts our spirituality. Holiness is for everyone, so there has to be a way for average men and women to grow in their walk with Christ, without having to pretend we are living in a convent or monastery centuries removed from our present and hectic moment.

How can parents have a spirituality that is thriving, even abundant? How can busy professionals walk closer to God even when the demands of work are all-consuming? Answering these questions is the reason for this book.

There are thirty chapters, each of which deals with a primary spiritual point. I suggest you progress from start to finish, simply reading and thinking about the content of one chapter per day. This in some ways is a makeshift retreat for the person who just can't participate in that coveted month-long silent journey that promises renewal or even make a weekend retreat.

There are many ways we can encounter Christ, and we all have unique responsibilities, trials, histories, and expectations. So the journey to God will be a bit different for each of us. I know that God wants to meet us, even in our brokenness, and bring us into abundant living. We are all capable of being saints, even if we have children going to the public school instead of the private, or if we shop at the mall, and get our java at a certain coffee shop with a mermaid-siren for its logo.

So for thirty days I want you to relax and take a good look at where you are in your spiritual journey. Are you nearer to God now than you were a few years ago? Or do you feel as if you've lost hope amid the chaos of your daily routine? Assess your situation, and beg for the grace to truly grow in Christ. God wants you to encounter him even more than you desire to find him!

This book is for people like you and me: people in the world but not wanting to be of it (see John 17:11–19). For you who wonder if you can still be spiritual as you deal with life's daily grind, my hope is that this book will give you victory and coping mechanisms in areas you feel are beyond remedy.

Enjoy your next thirty days with this book. May you realize that Mary is pouring the graces of her Son in your life, enabling you to will the good over the average in every moment.

chapter 1

There Must Be More to Life

*T*here must be more to life than work and entertainment. Dreaming of retirement, winning the lottery, becoming the next American Idol, entertaining ourselves to death—where's the substance? Deep inside, every person wants to live life to the full, but what that might look like or how it might be achieved is a mystery to many.

Is it possible that if we stopped to examine our lives, we'd find we are not living the fullest life possible? How do we counter the mundane with authenticity? How do we achieve true meaning in our present moment?

The key to unfolding a deeper way of living is a thriving spirituality. This is the path that gives us some answers and brings us to fulfillment.

Spirituality is a loaded word these days, meaning different things to different people. It has many expressions throughout the world and leads individuals down different avenues. In this book I'm talking about specifically Catholic spirituality. The Christian faith allows us the greatest opportunity for a truly meaningful life.

Many Christians have some type of lived spirituality. People might not feel that they're living the abundant life Jesus promises, but they probably believe that certain practices will bring that goal within reach. Many contemporary spiritual books tell us to go to Mass, pray the rosary, and feed the hungry. But these right actions—even when performed with sincere motivation—can grow old, and we often lack the will to persevere.

Will we live more abundantly if we get up at 5:30 AM so we can pray for three hours? What if we drift off to sleep after five minutes? How can we be spiritual when we can only get to the book of Leviticus in our annual attempt to read the Bible from beginning to end?

Is there really a spirituality we can live with—not just endure? Is there a spirituality that will help us to live life abundantly? How can we unfold habits of holiness that we can actually maintain?

Many saints and other spiritual people had extended graces that we'll never have and disciplines that seem other-worldly. And here we stand, simple and unfit for anything truly dynamic. Seemingly impossible expectations present a big problem: We will never be able to do what appears to be expected of us, so we fall into feelings of inadequacy, spiritual bankruptcy, and even guilt. But God extends his graces to everyone, not just to nuns and priests and people who seem to have it all together.

Certain styles in spiritual movements come and go. But there are a few practices that have worked for me regardless of where I have been in life. I feel confident in these avenues of holiness, having found them expressed in sacred Scripture, Church teachings, and the lives of the saints. For example, you can never negate the importance of the sacraments.

Having a foundation of proven spiritual practices is important, and yes, there are some that will always be there for us. Over time, if not now, these essentials of Catholic spirituality will make practical sense to you. In the rest of this book, we're going to look at many of these building blocks, so that you can put together a firm foundation for a vibrant spiritual life.

But first ask yourself, where am I in terms of the abundant life?

Consider this: The human person is both spirit and body, and while certain spiritualities have emphasized one over the other, authentic Christianity sees the body as a needed expression of the spirit, and the spirit as a life-giving reality in relation to the body. I remember the first time I saw a corpse. I knew the man in life as vibrant, energetic, and extremely intense. After his spirit had left, that body seemed to be missing the reality of who he was: His "me-ness" was no longer there, even though the shell of his body remained.

On the other hand, I have seen countless people who seem to be walking, talking zombies. These "living dead" have bodies with a pulse, but their spirit is lifeless within. And then there are those who are nearly dead physically but whose spirits are vibrant and flowing. St. Padre Pio bore the stigmata, the wounds of the crucified Jesus, yet there was a brightness and life to this tattered priest.

Most of us are somewhere in the middle of these two extremes: We are not dead spiritually, but we are not living a rich, fruitful life. We have good days and bad, moments of spiritual clarity and times when we're stuck in neutral. God wants to meet us where we are—broken, apathetic, tired, whatever—to heal us and bring us into an abundant life. He doesn't want us to keep reaching but never attaining—that isn't spirituality, that's a path toward the eventual collapse of our will and our dreams.

If we're still breathing, God is giving us the time we need to truly be given over to him.

Before you go on with this book, think about your relationship with God and your efforts to connect spiritually. Having a sense of where you are will help you as you move toward where you want to be. And remember, God isn't done with you yet.

For Reflection

1. Do you feel nearer to God now than you did a few years ago? If not, list some circumstances, experiences, fears, or distractions that might be contributing to your sense of distance.

2. Have you found certain spiritual practices, books, discussion groups, blogs, music, or chat rooms useful connections with your faith? What was it about those things that drew you out of yourself?

3. Consider the means God has used to touch you in the past, so that you can think about the role these can play as you work toward a spirituality you can live with.

chapter 2

It's All About Relationship

While recognizing that we are all at different places on our spiritual journey, there are some general truths we can and must understand. The first is quite obvious but bears saying: Spirituality is about a relationship with Jesus—not regulations. Christianity has always been about the person of Christ—his life, death, and resurrection.

Religion is an attempt by the human person to answer primordial questions, such as who am I and why do I exist.[1] Many religions have facets of beauty and goodness and truth that benefit their followers' relationships with self and others, but Christianity is the greatest answer to these primordial questions, because it is centered on the person of Jesus Christ, who is "the way, and the truth, and the life" (John 14:6).[2] He is the Word given in response to our great queries.

"Who do you say that I am?" (Mark 8:29) is a question that demands a response from each of us because it has eternal consequences. If we say that Jesus is truly the God-man, then we owe him our allegiance and our very lives. C.S. Lewis posed this thought in *Mere Christianity*:

> A man who was merely a man and said the sort of things Jesus said would not be a great moral teacher. He

would either be a lunatic—on a level with the man who says he is a poached egg—or else he would be the Devil of Hell. You must make your choice. Either this man was, and is, the Son of God, or else a madman or something worse. You can shut Him up for a fool, you can spit at Him and kill Him as a demon; or you can fall at His feet and call Him Lord and God. But let us not come with any patronizing nonsense about His being a great human teacher. He has not left that open to us.[3]

Jesus shows us how to be fully human. All deity and all human, he shows us that a truly complete person is one who is in a life-giving relationship with God and others. Recollect Jesus' constant dialogue with the Father and his willingness to share himself with those he met, whether they were broken, unclean, or successful.

We are not hired servants or slaves, nor are we simply tolerated by Christ; rather, we are loved! Sacred Scripture tells us, "We love, because he first loved us" (1 John 4:19). Christ entered into time to demonstrate God's great love for us. He loved the woman at the well, and he loved Peter in his brokenness, asking him, "Do you love me?" (see John 4:4–42; 21:15–19). Jesus loved Zacchaeus, acknowledging this sinner as a person worthy of fellowship, and he invited the woman caught in adultery to go and sin no more (Luke 19:2–10; John 8:3–11).

Christ invites us, too, into a relationship of love. His love is gentle and self-controlled, keeps no record of wrong, and believes and hopes all things (see 1 Corinthians 13:4—13). The relational love of Christ empowers. "For the love of Christ urges us on, because we are convinced that one has died for all" (1 Corinthians 5:14).

Knowing that the Second Person of the Blessed Trinity became man allows us to reconsider that which we are: flesh and spirit. We are not asked to be mythically in Christ, as if it were some sort of mental state of being. In all actuality we, through baptism, are now truly placed in Jesus. "You have come to fullness of life in him, who is the head of all rule and authority" (Colossians 2:10).

St. Paul says in Galatians 2:20 that it isn't he who lives any longer; rather Christ lives in him. This is why we can walk in abundant living. Christ in us does not negate our unique personality, nor does he eliminate our singular contribution to the human experience. The opposite is true: Christ in us enables us to be the fullest and most authentic versions of ourselves.

A relationship with Jesus is the basis of a spirituality that we can and must live. Christ is the fulfillment of all that we long for. He cries out, "Come to me, all who labor and are heavy laden, and I will give you rest" (Matthew 11:28). Come and rest then, and be the person you were created to be.

For Reflection
1. Have you answered for yourself the question Christ posed: "Who do you say that I am?" What conclusions have you come to?
2. Have there been times in your life when you have seen or felt Christ's love for you? How did those experiences change or validate your faith?
3. If you have not experienced Christ's love, ask him to show himself to you. And ask him to open your eyes so you can see his great love for you.

chapter 3

Brokenness: The Upside to the Downside

We as a culture and even a nation are not interested in brokenness. Our role models are those who are wealthy and secure, famous and beautiful. Our heroes are at the top of their game, whether in music, theater, cinema, sports, or any other profession. We want our leaders to be above the fray.

What happens when those who seemed untouchable fail? We vilify them and run as far as possible from their brokenness. Individually and as a society, we fixate on others' pain to divert attention from our own brokenness.

We judge others more harshly when their personal choices contribute to their state of brokenness. In contrast, individuals whose circumstances are beyond their control elicit sympathy and even practical help. But in both scenarios we are afraid of the brokenness we see. They shatter our notions of security: Wealth and fame cannot protect an individual from poor choices, and none of us are safe from that which is beyond our control.

In finding a livable spirituality, we must first acknowledge our brokenness. This concept may seem a bit ironic and difficult to comprehend, because it goes against everything we're conditioned to believe about greatness. We are afraid to be vulnerable about our struggles. In fact, in our formative years we learn tactics for keeping a protective exterior in place. We learn that being made fun of is a humiliation to avoid. We hear comments that sink deep within our spirits, so we toughen up lest we be destroyed. But this often leaves our hearts hardened.

Our culture tells us to run from our brokenness—to prepare, educate, analyze, and will ourselves into healing. We might attend self-help lectures, collect gurus with new and innovative ideologies, or accrue wealth as a cover. And yet we remain broken. The world can't provide the answer. We must confront the glaring reality that we are unable to achieve true rest and lasting joy on our own.

Many of us have experienced brokenness because of our own sin or that of others. In the struggle against the world, the flesh, and the devil, there are casualties. The world promises joy it can't deliver. When we bow to the cravings of the flesh, temporary happiness leads to bondage rather than lasting rest. The enemy comes to steal, kill, and destroy (see John 10:10). We either grow bitter in our brokenness or embrace the healing presence of Christ in our deepest wounds.

I was about five years old when my parents took my sister and me to my grandparents' for a Christmas I'll never forget. These gatherings were always special. My grandmother was particularly sensitive to what would encourage young kids: lots of candy and television and learning how to gamble for dimes and nickels while playing rummy. But what made this particular Christmas vacation stand out was that my father took me aside and knelt down to deliver an important message to my little mind. He said, "I won't be there when you get home." I had no idea what he meant.

My father and mother had gotten to a place in their relationship where things couldn't be resolved. I know that my dad didn't want to hurt my sister and me, but his choice to begin another life outside of our family was a great source of brokenness in my life. It impacted my perception of God as Father and led to all sorts of difficulties.

I encounter young people and adults all over the world who are still trying to come to grips with broken areas of their lives. Perhaps a family member died or left, or perhaps the person lived with abuse and belittlement. One of the frustrations we must recognize is that we pass our brokenness on to others. My father was broken, having lost his father during his teens. His departure certainly left many questions as to what my life as a husband and father might look like, and I know I have passed on some of my brokenness to my children.

However we arrive at brokenness, acknowledging that we are broken is of the utmost importance when it comes to spiritual growth. Brokenness enables us to truly be humble, which in turn enables us to look for help. Christ said that the meek shall inherit the earth and that he came to call sinners, not the righteous (see Matthew 5:5; 9:13). His invitation is to come to him in our brokenness, and in him we will find true fulfillment and satisfaction. "The LORD is near to the brokenhearted, and saves the crushed in spirit" (Psalm 34:18).

I thank God for his saving grace in my life. During the initial time of my family's brokenness, my mother began to take my sister and me to church on a regular basis. The cliché "Christianity is just a crutch" was certainly applicable to us, for we were a broken family in need of great healing. We found that Christ was present for us, and this enabled us to take steps that seemed impossible. Thankfully my dad and I have a wonderful relationship now, which has also assisted in healing the broken areas of my life.

God has ways of fixing things when we cannot fix ourselves. Spiritual brokenness is recognizing that we need our Savior. It is an acute awareness of our need for joy and rest in our struggle against the world, the flesh, and the devil. We will face this primordial three-faceted struggle until we cross over into eternity. Only the Lord can enable us to do battle successfully; only he can bind up our wounds and heal our battle scars. True joy and peace are on the straight and narrow path that Jesus shows us.

For Reflection

1. Have you experienced brokenness in your life? Are you bitter or better because of it?
2. Have you witnessed brokenness in another individual that caused you to be fearful? What about that brokenness made you afraid?

chapter 4

Weakness Needs a Helping Hand

S t. Paul says to the Corinthians, "I will all the more gladly boast of my weaknesses, that the power of Christ may rest upon me. For the sake of Christ, then, I am content with weaknesses, insults, hardships, persecutions, and calamities; for when I am weak, then I am strong" (2 Corinthians 12:9–10).

Our weakness is not a great surprise when we are honest with ourselves. Often it is in confronting our brokenness that we discover how weak we are. That's what happened in my broken family. We realized that we didn't have the ability to fix ourselves.

Believe me, I tried desperately to figure out ways to get my father and mother back together. I would pray, believing that Jesus heard the prayers of little children, but still my parents couldn't find a way to resolve their brokenness.

Weakness is similar to brokenness in some ways. We might spend the greater part of our lives trying to pretend we are strong when we are not. We try to be self-sufficient, associating weakness with fragility. On the other hand, admitting our weakness—admitting that we are unable to put things back together on our own—can take us to a place of healing and authentic strength. Amid my family's difficulties we did more than merely survive; we became strong.

What does it mean to be weak? It certainly means that we are in need. When as humans are we most in need? When we are children. Jesus even tells us to be childlike (see Mark 10:14–15). It is when we are children that we don't hesitate to ask for assistance.

This invites humility, the awareness that we are unfit or unable to proceed without assistance.

If I cannot do a specific number of pull-ups, it may be that I am too weak physically to qualify for the Navy Seals or some other profession; simply put, I may be unfit for the task. A weak moral character has more negative connotations: It perhaps indicates a person's willing something less than what he or she is capable of. A person who chooses to give a halfhearted effort to a task at hand would be considered weak.

Weakness in spirituality is where the most definitive expression of strength occurs. Why? Because it is a place of humility, in which the individual fully depends upon the Lord instead of self. The Office of Readings reminds us that we need assistance for spiritual growth: "God, come to my assistance. Lord, make haste to help me."[1]

This last year I started running, which was a surprise even to myself. I had always thought that if I had time to exercise, I had better use it to write another book or song, schedule another speaking engagement, or do something else that would help me make a living. Exercise didn't seem to be "me." But I got into it, and I completed my first half-marathon at the beginning of May.

As the summer months rolled around, I wanted to continue my regular runs, but the heat was overwhelming. One day I went out mid-afternoon. The route was shadeless and the weather humid. At the sixth mile (which was to be my last), I started to get dizzy and felt out of sorts. I leaned over to catch my breath and downed the last bits of my replenishment liquid. In a couple minutes I felt calm and able to move.

This is a clear picture of what weakness looks like and what help looks like. In order for me to get to my final destination, I needed to be refreshed and replenished. We all need that in our spiritual journey. So let's rely on the Lord in our weakness. He supplies all the graces we need.

For Reflection

1. In what areas of your life—such as your physical life, family life, career, and spiritual life—have you been taken past your natural abilities and enabled to identify your weaknesses? What are those weaknesses?
2. What are you doing with your weaknesses? Where do you feel they are taking you?

chapter 5

Emptied to Be Filled

*I*n brokenness we want to heal, in weakness we want to be strong, but only in emptiness can our brokenness and weakness be dealt with. This emptiness is not a desire for nothingness as an end in itself; this is not nirvana. Rather it is being entirely empty of our wants, even empty of our desire to try again, recognizing our true need for God in all areas. Emptiness given to Christ becomes life-giving; emptiness without Christ leads to despair and hopelessness. Emptiness given to Christ allows us to finally be filled!

How do we pass into emptiness? By accepting the fact that we can't fix ourselves or be strong on our own. It is difficult to change ourselves. In emptiness we open our lives to be filled with Christ. This is where we begin to finally receive healing.

We empty ourselves of our wants, desires, and passions in order to align ourselves with the One who truly knows and loves us. We empty ourselves of the temptations of the world, the demands of the self, and the distractions of the devil, in order to be filled with the love Christ has for us and for the whole world. When we are empty we can truly be filled with Christ.

St. John says, "He who is in you is greater than he who is in the world" (1 John 4:4), and Paul speaks of "Christ in you, the hope of glory" (Colossians 1:27). These passages express the recognition of our being in Christ, which enables us to truly walk as we are called to walk. Galatians 5:16 says, "[W]alk by the Spirit, and do not gratify the desires of the flesh." A spirituality we can live with is a spirituality that works!

The story of the widow's mite exemplifies this situation (see Luke 21:1–4). The widow gave all she had to God, and it was in this total gift, in her being entirely empty, that she drew the attention of God. Why did her willingness to give all impress Jesus? Because it was a picture of God's love in time. We should be in a continual place of emptiness, always leaving room for God to fill that which we have entirely given to him.

Everyone is going to be broken, and everyone will be brought to a point of weakness through that brokenness. The question arises, what do we do with this brokenness and this inability to heal ourselves?

This place of brokenness and weakness can be frightening. Many young people find themselves without hope, unable to see a reason to keep on living. Countering this momentum is part of the reason I do what I do.

A number of years ago a girl approached me at the end of one of my talks and nervously said that she wanted to share with me something of great importance. I've never forgotten what she said: "I have the razor blades in my room."

I only had a few minutes before they would call me back on stage. I stood there dumbfounded. Was I hearing her correctly?

I said, "If no one else tells you, I want you to know that you matter. You matter to me." And then I told her that if she did something stupid like try to kill herself, I'd kill her. She smiled.

This was a haunting moment for me, as I looked into the eyes of this poor young girl who lived in a constant state of emptiness. For her, life seemed pointless. She did not feel valuable, beautiful, or wonderful.

Some people choose to stay in their emptiness and die there. But we are not to stop in spiritual paralysis. In order to come fully to spiritual life and growth, we must face our emptiness and surrender to the Father. Then we can be filled with Christ, the only one who can heal and strengthen.

Jesus' agony in Gethsemane, the denial and betrayal of his friends, the beatings, the insults, and the blows left him broken. Jesus modeled weakness in crying out to the Father that this cup be taken from him, though not according to his will but the Father's (see Luke 22:42). Christ Jesus emptied himself of anything but the Father's will and thus was able to bring life to all who brought about his brokenness. This act of complete self-donation enables us now to bring our brokenness to Golgotha, where we die spiritually in our weakness, knowing that our eventual emptiness is the conduit of authentic life!

Emptiness is a means to sanctity. I can take my frustration at being weak and broken, let it go, and let Christ create a new person out of me.

> My Lord God, I have no idea where I am going. I do not see the road ahead of me.
>
> I cannot know for certain where it will end. Nor do I really know myself, and the fact that I think that I am following your will does not mean that I am actually doing so. But I believe that the desire to please you does in fact please you. And I hope I have that desire in all that I am doing. I hope that I will never do anything

apart from that desire. And I know that if I do this you will lead me by the right road though I may know nothing about it. Therefore will I trust you always though I may seem to be lost and in the shadow of death. I will not fear, for you are ever with me, and you will never leave me to face my perils alone.

—Thomas Merton[1]

For Reflection
1. Are you afraid to be empty? Why?
2. What areas of weakness do you need to surrender to the will of God, in order to empty yourself and prepare for his renewal?
3. How can a place of emptiness allow you to walk in victory?

chapter 6

God's Love Poured Out: The Trinitarian Perspective

*T*he Trinitarian perspective might seem to be a daunting topic for a book on livable spirituality, but I am confident that God is patient with us as we seek to understand more about him. My son Kolbe has helped me see this more clearly.

When Kolbe was small, maybe a little under three, his sister gave him a Skittle candy. As he walked away, Kolbe began to tap his chest. I asked his sister, "Sarah, did Kolbe just make the Sign of the Cross after he received a Skittle?" She didn't know, so I had her call him back and give him another candy.

Sure enough, upon receiving the candy, Kolbe walked away tapping his chest, as if he'd just received the Eucharist at Mass. Part of me wanted to yell out that it was just candy, yet I realized that this was his way of putting into practice what he'd been witnessing at Mass. Eventually Kolbe learned the difference between the Eucharist and the Skittle, as is expected with proper catechesis and age.

In some ways I see this as an image of what happens to us as we journey closer to God. We may not fully understand everything yet, but we will grow in our faith over time and be able to distinguish and clarify what is necessary.

Our faith is Trinitarian, and understanding this One God in three Persons will ground our spirituality in truth. But when our parish priest spoke about the Trinity once, he quoted a line from St. Thomas Aquinas to the effect that, if one discusses the Trinity for more than an hour, he is likely to commit heresy. I'll keep it brief.

We are striving to be entirely open to God's love poured out for us in time. This is difficult to understand, let alone apply in our daily lives. The Trinity is going to give us a better picture of how we are to receive love; however, our finite comprehension of God as love will pale in comparison to the reality. Thankfully God has revealed himself to us in two ways. First, through natural law, and second, through divine revelation.

Natural law opens our eyes to a Creator. We see the magnificence of the creation around us, the diversity of the human person, the complexity of space and time, and they all point our attention "up." God has also revealed himself to us beyond what we can gather on our own efforts—through the covenants, patriarchs, prophets, and ultimately the Second Person of the Blessed Trinity. Jesus is the fullness of God's revelation. And he sends the Holy Spirit. We need the Trinity.

The reality of the Trinity as a family is truer than the representations we see on earth (though the sacrament of marriage should model this, as the spouses become complete gifts to one another, open to life). Each Person of the Most Holy Trinity is lacking in nothing. As the Father completely donates himself to the Son in the love of the Holy Spirit, the Son entirely pours himself out in the love of the same Holy Spirit back to the Father.

The best way to comprehend the entire and total love of the Trinity is Christ Jesus' complete gift of self to the Father in the love of the Holy Spirit at Calvary. Here Jesus willingly offers himself as a life-giving gift, including the brokenness, weakness, and emptiness of those who have nailed him to the cross.

Even Jesus' incarnation is an expression of self-emptying (*kenosis*) for the purpose of showing us how to love the Father. St. Paul tells the Philippians, "Have this mind among yourselves, which was in Christ Jesus, who, though he was in the form of God, did not count equality with God a thing to be grasped, but emptied himself, taking the form of a servant, being born in the likeness of men. And being found in human form he humbled himself and became obedient unto death, even death on a cross" (Philippians 2:5–8). This total gift to us in the Incarnation is brought to completion in Jesus' self-donation to the Father on Calvary, in the love of the Holy Spirit.

We are called to this type of love. We are invited to offer ourselves back to God as total gift. Yes, this includes suffering, sometimes great suffering. Jesus even said that love was intrinsically tied to laying one's life down for another: "Greater love has no man than this, that a man lay down his life for his friends" (John 15:13).

Why is there no greater love? Because this is the complete gift of self that will most model in time the eternal love of the Trinity.

For Reflection

1. Think about the Trinity as complete gift from one Person to the next. How does Christ model this in time? How can you be a gift to others?

2. How has God revealed himself to you in what you see around you? How have you grown in your understanding of God because of this?

chapter 7

Who Are You?

Who we are matters in regard to our spirituality.

If you are gregarious and the life of the party, it is understandable that your spirituality may express itself outwardly. If you long to be silent, hidden, and quiet, then your introversion may be a gift enabling you to come closer to Christ. You don't want to pretend to be someone that you are not, for authentic spirituality is honest to the gift of who you are as a human person.

To walk aound in a state of scholarly seriousness would just not be what I am about. I laugh easily, I feel deeply, and I remember moments that many forget simply because they make me smile. God made me this way, and I thank him for that. When I was a kid, I spent a lot of time in after-school detention. For what, you may ask? I couldn't stop talking in class. I loved making my friends laugh with stories that centered on classic boy themes such as blood, boogers, farts, weapons, sports—and did I mention blood? Telling how I got a scar or miscalculated a jump over hay bales was great fun. But my humor didn't endear me to my teachers.

My love for storytelling and making others laugh continued through junior high and high school and college. When I began speaking and performing music before audiences, my talent for entertainment was finally put to good use. I've often wanted to gather all of my teachers together and say to them, "While my timing may have been a bit off, people pay me a lot of money to make them laugh now." Of course, I'd never say that (only write it in a book), and I probably deserved every disciplinary action given to me. But I love the fact that God called me to do something that fits the talents he gave me.

Extroverts and introverts must learn from each other. For example, introverts need to be pressed to live their spirituality in a way that impacts the world. They are called to love others, to touch the proverbial neighbor, even as a monk or a cloistered nun. Such an impact is a must in authentic spiritual expression, because we are not singular in our walk with and toward Christ.

Extroverts, on the other hand, must find a way to be silent. They need to develop the willingness to enter into solitude in order to deepen their walk with Christ. In the end they will also make a stronger impact on those with whom they long to interact. Even Jesus spent time alone in prayer.

Family also affects who we are and our ability to respond to God. We are all born into this life from the intimate act (ideally loving and sacramental) of a man and a woman. When a family is a place of complete gift, where a father and mother willingly lay their wants and plans down for the betterment of one another and their children, we see an authentic expression of what God does for us in the person of Jesus Christ at Calvary. When a child lovingly responds to this pouring forth of self, this imitates Christ's gift to the Father in the love of the Holy Spirit. The family unit can model the Trinity and thus powerfully impact its members spiritually.

My grandparents were wonderful models for me in this area. Whenever I had a need or a want, my grandparents were more than happy to bless me. They certainly didn't do this because they had to; rather they loved to generously pour into my life their time, talents, and money. They wanted to bless me because my existence was a blessing to them.

If our familial surroundings are messed up, then we may need to work through some misinformation concerning who we think God is. The primary reality of his being father might be awkward to our reality if our own father has left us, passed away, or never involved himself in family life. We see Christ as our elder brother and those in the Church as brothers and sisters in the faith, but this perspective can be terribly battered if our siblings have hurt us repeatedly over the years. It's good to be aware of this so we can pursue healing in this area.

Friends can be incredible sources of healing and even spiritual guides. By *friend* I mean someone who is there for you even when you are irritable, grumpy, or emotional—in other words, at your worst. Jesus talks about true friendship as laying down your life for another (see John 15:13). Such sacrificial friendships can point us toward the beauty of being in a relationship with God.

My wife, Linda, benefitted from the faithful spiritual witness of her college roommate. Julie would wake up early to read Scripture and spend time in prayer every day. This faithfulness and quiet witness sparked a desire within Linda to move from selfishness to selflessness. And that completely changed her life and mine.

God has formed you in many ways. He gave you a particular personality and temperament; he blessed you with certain gifts; he put you in your unique family and has led you to teachers, friends, pastors, and other spiritual guides. All of this bears on your identity and your calling. So it bears asking, who are you?

For Reflection
1. Are you an introvert, an extrovert, or somewhere in the middle? Do you meet God in solitude, in community, or both?
2. Did your upbringing help or hinder your spiritual growth?
3. Are there people in your life who call you on to a deeper walk with Christ? If not, how might you develop such relationships?

chapter 8

Where Are You?

The call on your life matters when considering your spirituality. Your vocation is the avenue by which you fulfill your mission, purpose, and calling in life. In fact, the Latin word *vocare* means "to call."

God calls each of us to be saints, to love and be loved. Finding our vocation and knowing our personality within that vocation help define our spirituality. Two religious sisters can be noticeably different in how they live this out, because within each vocation we are all different. Walking in the vocation we have been called to by God will allow us to make the greatest impact.

I was at the final Mass of a Steubenville youth conference for which I had been a speaker. After this liturgy there is always an "altar call" for those who sense that God is leading them into the religious life, whether as a sister, a brother, or a priest. My family was with me for the Mass, and I tried to explain to my kids what was going on.

My five-year-old son, Jude, was somewhat insistent that he go up for the priestly calling. Not wanting him to go alone, I asked his brother Kolbe to accompany him. As they moved toward the collection of young men up in front, my four-year-old son, Joseph, began to whine, "I want to go to the bathroom too."

I said to Joe, "They are not going to the bathroom. They are going up to consider the possibility of being a priest one day."

Joseph then began to whine, "I want to be a priest too." So I told him to follow his brothers.

As they settled back into their seats after the prayer, Kolbe asked, "What was that?" It made me smile.

When we talk about the importance of vocation, God isn't about to dupe you into anything. In the end, it isn't as if you'll be able to say, "What was that?" Vocation is something we get to have an active part in. God is looking for our yes.

Whether you are young or elderly or anywhere in between, God has called you to walk in love. Look at who and where you are right now. Are you walking in the vocation that God has for you?

Traditionally we recognize marriage, holy orders, religious life, and consecrated celibacy as vocations. Most people end up married, and that vocation is actually a sacrament that reflects Christ's love for the Church. Priests and religious are married to the Church or to Christ himself, and their journey toward sanctity is best found along this path. All of these are holy calls. Knowing more about how God calls and uses people will assist you in finding out how to live your spirituality.

Maybe you are a mom with six children who does three loads of laundry a day, or maybe you teach at a public school. Maybe you are just beginning your life as an adult, or maybe you have been married for forty years to the same person. Possibly you are facing difficulties this year unlike any you've ever encountered, or maybe this is just another year of the exact same dynamics as the previous one. Look at where you are and realize that your spirituality is meant to impact the environment in which you move, work, and live.

It is impossible for spirituality to be authentic and as effective as it should be if you wish you were someone else, lived somewhere else, or had something else. You must really find a way to be where you are. To bloom where you are planted enables you to truly be. To be what? To be Christ—to be his love, patience, generosity, and all that he is. True spirituality is to be lived, not imagined!

I am not sure why this happens, but many minds throughout the world come to a skewed idea of what true spirituality looks and acts like. Let's use a mother of four as an example. This mother reads a book by St. Thérèse and suddenly thinks she needs to have a certain number of hours in prayer each day. She must get away from the chaos of everyday life in order to be a saint. The reality is that this mother is not a cloistered nun living in France a hundred or so years ago. She is not as young as St. Thérèse and certainly not able to have her day regimented in the way the Carmelites did in Lisieux, nor does she even have the ability to spend that much time in silence. This mom's thought of applying the rhythm of a nun's life to the reality of motherhood is a recipe for disaster, both for mom and family! It is a plan of insanity that will either drive her to spiritual exhaustion, hopelessness, and defeat or drive everyone around her nuts!

Think of a father who reads the life of St. Francis and now wants to give away all of his household items, eat table scraps, and practice severe penance. After all, St. Francis was a great man after God's heart. He certainly was a wonderful man, and we can learn a lot from him, but Francis was not a father. He became the fullness of who *he* could be. He was himself, as we are to be the best versions of ourselves.

Moms and dads are not called to the rhyme and rhythm of a priest, sister, religious, or even the single life. Married couples have a spirituality that is consistent with being married; and that can even change with the coming of children. If you are a father, your spirituality has to include your wife and kids. If you are a mother, you need to remember that your primary vocation is to get your spouse and your kids to heaven. How that will look is going to be different for every family and individual, but there are some given principles that will work.

We all have much to learn from the saints, but we must apply their lessons within the context of our vocations and our unique spiritual journeys. St. Thérèse is a doctor of the Church, which means that her teaching is applicable to us all in a very important way. We can certainly follow her "little way of spiritual childhood," which means doing little things with great love. It will mean joyfully carpooling, doing your best at work every day and being patient with your coworkers, speaking gently to a sibling who is annoying, answering a child's question with patience, and praying for those irritating neighbors. It may look a little different each day, but the principle of loving greatly in the smallest things is one that can and does work! It is a spirituality you can live.

You are not at this moment the final version of yourself: You are still growing spiritually. Be assured that God is faithful and will finish what he has started in you (see Philippians 1:6). You are on a journey toward becoming a person of deep spirituality. Keep in mind that it is a journey that will not be completed until you reach heaven. You will not begin your journey toward sanctity where St. Thérèse ended hers. Be patient with yourself.

For Reflection

1. What is your vocation? What is the current context in which you must live your unique spirituality?
2. Is there a specific saint whose spirituality touches your life? How can you apply that spirituality in the context of your life?

chapter 9

Who Is Your Neighbor?

One thing that we cannot forget in our endeavor toward a spirituality we can live with is the call to love our neighbor. Yes, you want to find your spirituality, but the purpose of that is to love God, and "he who does not love his brother whom he has seen, cannot love God whom he has not seen" (1 John 4:20). We must reach out to others, not exclude or judge them. As you grow in the knowledge of who Jesus is and what he has done, you will become more like him: You will be present to those in need. A deepening spirituality must include the other.

We have a tendency to categorize one another. If we can put people into a box or stereotype them, we don't have to spend time truly getting to know them. They are either liberal or conservative, Democrat or Republican, charismatic or traditional; the list goes on and on. It's safer that way. However, God doesn't want us to be safe; he wants us to be saints!

There are a few vagrant adults who benefit from traditional Catholic guilt by arriving at our parish church just before or just after Mass. They are not homeless; rather they wander about during the day before gathering at one of the many halfway houses and adult living centers in our area. There is a particular man whom I tell regularly that I will not give him money, but if he is in fact hungry, I'll take him to get some food.

One day we were running late for Mass, and I was in no mood to talk to someone about his desire for extra change. As the man approached me with the typical request, I gave him my standard response, which he didn't care for. He mumbled something and huffed away, and I remember getting a bit steamed. After all, this wasn't the first time I'd told him the same thing. He just didn't get it.

My little girl was standing next to me, the rest of the family having already gone into church. She looked at the man walking away and then looked up at me and said, "I have money."

I was a bit dumbstruck, and I almost yelled out that she was in no way going to give that bum her money. But the Holy Spirit told me to be quiet and be sensitive to what was about to happen.

I asked my daughter if she wanted to give the man her money, and she just stared up at me. I took her little pink purse, reached in, and grabbed a dollar. I called the man back and tried to have a man-to-man conversation with him.

"My little girl is going to give you a dollar out of her own purse. Are you sure you need it?"

The man just stared at me, looking half-crazed, eager to take the money from this sweet little child. I gave him the money, and he walked off, not even thanking her.

I looked down at my daughter and realized I had witnessed something great. She was not interested in this man's past, what he would do with the money, or whether he deserved it. All she wanted to do was help him. It was the neighborly thing to do, and in fact, I'd say it was a heavenly thing that she did.

If Christ has a great love for all—in fact, if Christ holds all deep within himself—then Christ in us will enable us to love and hold all in our hearts. What would happen if we truly lived our spirituality with this truth at the forefront of our minds? We would most certainly treat those around us differently, because we would know, even if they are polar opposites to us in our beliefs and expressions, that they are nonetheless children of the God who radically receives and embraces us in our brokenness.

We don't want to fall into the trap of assuming that, after settling upon our vocation, we must now go out and do something or minister to a specific group. Rather we are called to touch the lives of those we encounter within the context of our vocation. We must love others right where they are. That disobedient child who sneaks out of the house, the elderly couple who complain about your crying infant at Mass, the friend who struggles with an eating disorder or drug addiction—all are on a journey toward spiritual awareness. We must pray for them, sacrifice, and serve them, and this has to be laced with love that is overflowing from our healed wounds. Authentic spirituality advances when we recognize that God has also called our neighbor into a holy vocation.

We can't give what we do not have. To truly minister to others, we must let Christ minister to us. To do otherwise is to step out on our own strength. Without the foundation of Christ's love in our lives, we have limited mercy to extend to those who are going through difficulties.

We've all been judged by others, and it never feels good, nor does it propel us into a deeper walk with Christ. This is oftentimes why people view Christianity in a negative light. They see a Church filled with hypocrites who judge rather than care for the broken. This happens when individuals attempt to move forward on their own strength rather than that of Jesus.

Why are we surprised that our friends are broken and weak? Why are we dumbfounded when a spiritual leader makes a monumental mistake? It is because we have looked at them as people who have previously won the trivial struggles with the flesh, are indifferent to the flow of the world, and are greater than the enemy. But in fact they are just like us—mortal.

The victories of spiritual leaders are not due to their individual efforts; that type of spirituality will not last. Rather their victories come, as do ours, from a continual awareness of the need for Christ as healer, victor, and compass. Simply put, we need to recognize that without Christ in our lives, we have no hope.

It is time to stop beating and killing our wounded. We have a vested interest in our neighbor's success. Jesus himself gives us the sobering picture of the final judgment, where the determining factor will be what we do for the other who is in need (see Matthew 25:31–46).

Jesus says we are in the world but are not to be of the world (see John 17:6–19). What are we of, if not of the world? We are now in Christ, we are in the family of God, and in fact, we are Jesus' body in time.

The standard for loving others may be greater than we've previously thought. Indeed, if Christ's laying his life down for friend and foe is the example of how we should treat each other, it stands to reason that we have a long way to go (see John 15:13).

For Reflection

1. Have you ever felt judged by others because your spiritual expression differed from theirs?

2. Who within the context of your vocation is in most need of Christ's love? How can you show that love?

3. Has Christ begun the healing process in you, so that you can reach out to others?

chapter 10

Living Your Love

*H*ow do we implement the truth of whose we are? How do we live an incarnational spirituality? This is what we must look at next.

Many Christians approach their spirituality with a sense of hopelessness. The idea of following a strict regimen may be appealing at first, but with the inconsistencies of daily life, the demands of raising a family, the continual driving to and from obligations, we can feel as if we are in survival mode rather than truly living the abundant life to which Jesus calls us (see John 10:10).

I often think we make spirituality harder than it really is. We think it is more about doing rather than being. So how do we change our thoughts? How do we put into the rhythm of a crazy life an authentic spirituality? In order to do this, we must review some remedial truths.

Living for Christ and in Christ is not a cerebral experience; it is an incarnational spirituality. This means that we live out in our daily lives the truths of who and whose we now are in Christ. Though deep considerations surrounding ideologies in spirituality are significant, ultimately our thinking must be manifested in our actions. The truth that we believe is the one we actually act on.

If we think about 1 Corinthians 13, we find the connection between action and motivation to be one of utmost importance. We may have incredible abilities in speaking, but without love we are a noisy gong or clanging symbol. We may even give our lives in martyrdom, but without love we gain nothing. Our actions must be soaked in love.

In the same way we cannot simply suggest another be warmed or filled without actually providing help in those areas (see James 2:15–17). Love is the motivation behind what we do for God. Without charity our acts are lifeless.

How do we make love the motivation behind what we do? We are broken, weak, and empty, yet Christ invites us to be in and of him. Our inclusion into the very life of God through baptism enables us to become what we could never have been otherwise. We are able to finally rest, to be at peace, to be persons filled with joy.

This walking about in the reality of who and whose we are is an incarnational expression. We recognize that we must love in thought, word, and action within our specific vocation in life, within the context in which we find ourselves at this moment. Living this life with authentic spirituality is not about what we can do for God as much as it is about springboarding into the moment with what he has done for us.

We cannot conjure up love by our own efforts, because then it just becomes one more thing on our already lengthy spiritual "to do" list. Finding ourselves in Christ, fully loved by the Father, receiving the Holy Spirit—who cries out within each of us, Abba—will be the foundation that enables our love to overflow to those around us. Simply put, you love because he first loved you! Think about it! And act upon it!

One Valentine's Day several years ago, my wife told me that she would like our children to make some cards and bring them to an assisted-living facility. I thought it was a delightful plan. My kids were excited, and they created mass quantities of cards decorated with hearts and sweet wishes, which of course the grandmothers and grandfathers would adore.

Then my wife wanted to know if I was planning to accompany them to the seniors' home. I was irritable about my list of things to do, which seemed to never end, and about the craziness of that particular day, so of course I didn't want to go. Yet I realized it would be the nice thing to do.

When I was a small boy, my great-grandmother was in an old folks' home, and we stopped by to visit her one summer afternoon. I remember the smell of the building was odd, with the scent of urine overwhelming any attempts of cleaning supplies. An elderly gentleman near the door wanted to shake my hand, which I willingly did with childlike innocence.

My family moved on down the hall, and I found that the old man wouldn't release my hand. He just moaned and shook my hand, each moment increasing my terror. I finally jerked free and was able to catch up with my father. My heart was racing with fear.

As I walked into the assisted-living facility with my family, I couldn't help but recall my childhood trauma, keeping an eye out for senior men in wheelchairs. My heart began to soften as I saw the joy on all of the elderly faces when given cards by children they had never met. It was special for all of us.

My three-year-old daughter handed the last card to a man in a wheelchair. The scratches and scrawls on the card were barely legible. If you've seen little children's drawings with a circle that is a head, sticks coming out for hands, lines dropping out the bottom for possible legs, then you have a pretty good idea of the card being presented to the man.

The man, however, made no move to take the gift. I reached over and put it on his chest, and he began to moan and rock a little. I stepped in front of my daughter in a protective gesture. I was a little irked that he didn't say thanks, and I wondered what his problem was.

It was then that I realized the man was unable to speak or even reach out to take the card. He was rocking back and forth with tears coming out of his eyes, moaning in gratitude. He'd obviously had a stroke (not from my children, mind you), and I knew that he was blessed by my little girl's gift.

This event taught me a lot about what love can look like. My daughter's gift did not need to be a great work of art to be priceless to that man that day. I realized that I was a part of something great, even though I'd come with such a poor attitude. God wants the little gifts that we have to be given freely, because he can do a lot with our yes.

A life fixated upon a job, money, or some other thing, however, leads only to selfishness, pride, fear, insecurities, anger, and a whole host of vices. The fruit is the result of an improper understanding of who we are. Meditating upon the good of a moment, the reality of who we are in Christ, will cause our minds to get into alignment with the truth. This belief will show up in our daily lives.

How do we focus on being loved by Christ? The Church has given us some tools: the Mass, adoration, sacramentals, and even good fellowship.

I can say that a chair will support my weight, but when I actually sit in that chair, I attest to that truth and rest upon it. This is true faith. Our actions will flow from our true faith. Our love for others will flow from our experiential love from Christ.

For Reflection

1. Are you engaged in any spiritual practices out of a sense of obligation rather than genuine appreciation for Christ?
2. How does being satisfied in Christ impact those around you? What are some practical ways you can see this happening?
3. Take a few moments to meditate on Christ and his love for you. What does that mean to you in your vocational expression?

chapter 11

God Chooses You!

*D*o you remember picking teams on the school playground? Usually the two most athletically capable individuals—perhaps the fifth-grade boys who had facial hair—were selected as captains. One of the most horrible moments for a young guy would be that of realizing that he stood a better than likely chance of being picked last. Usually this was some kid who had Coke-bottle glasses, his belt cinched up to his chest, and an IQ higher than that of most of the school's faculty. (This is the kid who will eventually employ the majority of the student body in his Fortune 500 company, although his high school career will be a living hell.)

When I was a boy, we played a ton of games on the playground—like Kill the Carrier, which was just an opportunity for us boys to beat each other up. For team games I was never a captain, and I was certainly never chosen first. But my best friends, Brad and Brian, were very coordinated, with amazing speed and basketball skills, and they were always chosen first.

The benefit I received was that I would be picked soon after they were. Even though I would stumble down the field gasping for breath, miss an easy shot, and let down the very people who picked me, I always managed to avoid being picked last because of the popularity and athleticism of my friends. They were a real safety net for me.

What I love about Christ is that he picks every one of us first. It is as if I were the only person on the playground.

God intentionally chose you to exist in time right now. Your existence may have been a surprise to even your parents, but to God your arrival was nothing less than his intention. The One we recognize as omnipotent (all-powerful), omnipresent (everywhere), and omniscient (all-knowing) has ordained your existence from all eternity. God planned you, with all of your unique idiosyncrasies and oddities, with all of your flaws, quirks, and mannerisms.

Your very existence says something profound about who God is. You are a singular and unique creative expression of a God who makes something out of nothing. This truth is transforming when you set your mind upon it.

The unique ways in which you read a poem, sing a song, laugh, speak, run, dance, or even breathe are gifts to all around you. There will never be another individual like you, nor has there ever been one with your singular qualities and peculiarities. Entirely your own, the very reality of your existence is a powerful witness to a world in need of surprises, a world that often considers life to be accidental or even a mistake.

You may spend hours wondering about your place in this world, and yet your existence is meant to be admired and, yes, even remembered. You may feel entirely average, with little to offer in comparison to the greatness of those around you, but remember, you have an impact that has consequences beyond what you can imagine.

The classic film *It's a Wonderful Life* is still popular because the truth it conveys resonates within us all: The world is a better place because of our existence. You may not realize how many lives you touch, nor will it seem your sacrifices and the dreams you've put on hold have meaning for anyone beyond a couple bystanders here and there; but in reality your existence impacts eternity. God not only planned your existence but also takes delight in how you see and process life around you. It is the joy of a Father toward his children, and we are all certainly his sons and daughters.

Just as my friends always had my back out there on the playground, God always wants you on his team. There is never a moment when he looks at you and wishes you were like someone else. You are worth more than you can imagine to God just because he loves you. You are valuable beyond compare because no one will ever be like you again. You are beautiful, and your existence says something powerful about a God who is radically involved in his creation. You are wonderful simply by taking in the next breath.

Because of God's love for you, he is preparing you to do something specific for his kingdom. Because of your uniqueness and singularity, the call upon your life is not simply to exist; rather it is to be the best possible version of yourself.[1] In other words, you are called to be a saint. God is committed to the reality of who you are and who you are becoming. Just as David's slaying of the lion and bear who came to destroy his sheep prepared him to face Goliath, so you are being prepared to destroy the Goliaths in your life (see 1 Samuel 17:34–36).

St. Paul wrote, "I am sure that he who began a good work in you will bring it to completion at the day of Jesus Christ" (Philippians 1:6). Our heavenly Father is faithful! He is entirely committed to your sanctity. He will not give up on you, because you are now in and part of Christ. Jesus is the vine; you are one of the branches (see John 15:5). He is the bread that has come from heaven (John 6:33–35), and as you eat the Body and drink the Blood of Christ, you are being conformed into his very image and likeness.

Your identification with God is a bodily one. Teresa of Avila said, "You are Christ's hands. Christ has no body now on earth but yours, no hands but yours, no feet but yours. Yours are the eyes through which Christ's compassion looks out on the world; yours are the feet with which he is to go about doing good; yours are the hands with which he is to bless men now."[2]

God invites us into fulfillment and prepares us to be what we are called to become. Lest we imagine our inabilities and failings to be too great, Jesus willingly died upon the cross, laying his life down for us. Your existence is worth his being spit upon, struck numerous times, whipped, mocked, ridiculed, and despised. You are worth every blow, every hateful comment, every nail, every thorn, and even death!

Having been buried with Christ in baptism (see Colossians 2:12), you are now one with God in his ultimate plan. He has chosen you and is preparing you to be like Christ to a world that is still in need of a Savior. You can now take upon yourself the mockery, ridicule, beatings, and betrayals, because Christ is in you.

The preparation is singular to you and your vocation. You can reach your family in a way that no one else can. You can reach your friends in a manner that others cannot. Remember, though, God's love for you is not contingent upon how many people you can reach. He embraces you not because you can do something for him but because he has done something for you.

This love the Father has for you will overflow to others. So you are truly prepared for ministry when you allow God to love you to the full. That love will allow you to look upon another person not as someone to be convinced, opposed, battled, or resisted but as someone whose very existence is singular and beautiful, whether the person realizes it or not. When all is said and done, this spirituality that one can live with is a spirituality that overflows from the realization of being loved!

With the insight of our being chosen and prepared to do great things should also come the awareness that we are in a battle. We have touched upon the primordial struggles that we have in this life with the world, the flesh, and the devil, but it is worth noting that these struggles are both active and passive. We face a culture that says a life of self-denial is ridiculous, and maybe we simply find it a little inconvenient to swim up that cultural stream, so to speak. But some of us meet active resistance, and some Christians even face martyrdom. From the times of Nero and Diocletian in Rome until today—in areas of China, Mexico, and other countries—to follow Christ means to battle a world entirely opposed to him.

The same is true for struggles against the flesh. Many of us regularly fight to reign in the appetites with some confidence; for others the battle seems impossible to win, so strong are the footholds the appetites have gained.

It is also the case that most of us do not encounter the devil in an explicit or physical way. We may think that the devil has infested our vehicles or is in cahoots with our difficult neighbors, but his presence is distant enough that we can imagine him as a figment of our imaginations rather than a true force to be contended with. Others have encountered the enemy in very physical ways. Padre Pio and other saints often sustained cuts and bruises from their battles with the evil one.

Whether in a minor or a major way, our struggles against these foes are real. Our job is not to muster up the courage to go into battle with our own strengths and strategies; rather it is to let Jesus protect and lead us! He may ask us to encounter "various trials" (James 1:2), but we know that he is with us and is doing a great work in our struggle. Although the enemy is like a roaring lion seeking whom he might devour (see 1 Peter 5:8), our God is greater: He is truly the victor! At the name of Jesus, every knee will bow and every tongue confess that Jesus is Lord (see Romans 14:11; Philippians 2:10). Let us cling to him in life's battles, crying out to the Lord of hosts.

God will protect us from our enemies; there is not a moment in this life when we are left to fend for ourselves. In fact, God gives us what we need for "life and godliness" (2 Peter 1:3). We have the armor of God, St. Paul says, with which to do battle (see Ephesians 6:10–18), for we are "God's chosen ones, holy and beloved" (Colossians 3:12).

For Reflection

1. Do you feel as if you have been specifically chosen by God to exist here in time? How has that impacted the way you view God and the way you view others?
2. What bears and lions from your past have enabled you to deal with Goliaths today? What do you think the victory over the current giants will look like?
3. How do you see God's protection demonstrated in your life?

chapter 12

Finding Solitude in the Chaos

Spirituality is not an end in itself. The point of spirituality is to realize God's love for us and let that love overflow to others.

Our spirituality is cyclical. Even though it is a place of dwelling in the love of the Trinity, it is also a deepening journey leading to greater clarity concerning this familial love. So how do we delve into this intimate love of the Trinity? We must cultivate silence and solitude. We need a sobering sense of our present moment, soaking in the beauty of each event with appreciation and satisfaction.

But alas, the world and its messages can rip any solitude from our hands before we realize it was even there. We have been conditioned to be distracted. The majority of us have not learned to be silent nor been trained to seize each moment as a gift.

From infancy we have been granted the privilege of continual distraction. Movement, music, and maternal affection enable our early years to be problem-free. As adolescents and teenagers we have technological distractions, playground experiences, and familial regimens. College students and young adults often use social gatherings and relationships to keep them from solitude—or alcohol to escape life's challenges. And as adults, distractions and difficulties abound: Family responsibilities and career pressures can stress even the most organized. So where in the mix of our daily routine can we experience and learn from solitude?

How can we calm ourselves amid the plethora of distractions?

Even should a moment of solitude come for us, our conditioning is such that our minds race, and our bodies become restless. The human person longs for the Sabbath rest, and the spirit longs for communion with the Father, but as Jesus told Peter in the Garden of Gethsemane, "the spirit indeed is willing, but the flesh is weak" (Matthew 26:41). The flesh will fight our pursuit of silence and solitude.

We certainly hear many distracting and demanding voices that press against the silence. As did Elijah, we must learn to hear God's true words in the "still, small voice" (1 Kings 19:12–13). God will speak to us about the reality of the moment and about where it can lead us, but we have to discern his word from the multiple words around us.

We are not to remain stagnant in a place that has offered renewal in the past; rather we press forward into the reality of our present and beyond. We had mutative transformations, you might say, at baptism, in which we received graces that had been lost due to original sin and that we certainly could not attain by ourselves. "Baptism ... makes the neophyte 'a new creature,' an adopted son of God, ... a 'partaker of the divine nature'" (*CCC*, 1265, 2 Corinthians 5:17; 2 Peter 1:4; see Galatians 4:5–7). All that we need for life and godliness is now granted to us in Christ (see 2 Peter 1:3). It is all gift, like an inheritance granted to the children of a wealthy father.

However, our ongoing and naturally unfolding spirituality is organic in its development. We gradually unpack the significance of who we are, with ever-increasing awareness.

Our heavenly Father grants to each of his children pearls of silence and solitude, so that we might enjoy his generosity.

Silence and solitude are the banquet that satisfies us and sustains our daily efforts. These quiet moments of renewal will lead us to touch others with what we have learned. Our meditations will show up in how we live.

When we focus upon the good, true, and beautiful, we have a chance to submit, even for a moment, to that which allows us spiritual clarity. Seizing small moments of beauty is a glass of water to a thirsty soul. Meditating upon spiritual words from the saints is savoring truth, which is a balm to our wounded consciences. Choosing the good over the mediocre raises our hearts to God's will.

It is important to seize each opportunity for beauty throughout the day, even if it is for only a second. That oasis may be the very gift you need to deal with the desert you are crossing.

Have you found him in the solitude?

That is a question to ask yourself in the context of who you are and where you are in life. The mother of four kids under six, the student with five major exams in three days, the father attempting to meet deadlines or client obligations can all cry out, What solitude? What silence? You have to be kidding!

And I will agree with you wholeheartedly. Finding time to be silent seems almost impossible for the mom and dad and student. So what is the solution?

What if the silence within a growing spirituality could be the five minutes you take in your car before walking into the office for the day, the fifteen minutes to quietly pray while you fall asleep at night, the four minutes in the restroom (that's where most mothers hide to get away from it all, isn't it?), or even the couple minutes before walking into your house after a busy day?

When added up, all of these pocket moments of silence can be great gifts in which to hear his voice.

Have you ever been driving down the road and suddenly realized, wow, I have no recollection of the last couple miles I drove. Why? Because you were so deep in thought that the driving was more autopilot than you'd care to admit.

Have you ever had to ask your spouse to repeat something because you were on a different planet with your thoughts? Wives, have you ever felt as if your husband wasn't really in the conversation? (OK, probably most of the time.)

The truth is, we are all experts at entering deep within to analyze a situation, think about a dilemma, or consider the odd comment of a peer. We might even enter la-la land to just think about the new fishing boat we want to get, the pitch that should have been delivered in the game, the catch that could have been made, and so on. We fade in and out of the regular daily chaos all of the time.

What I am suggesting is that there are times you can truly be in the moment while meditating upon the mysteries of our faith. You can move about your day attending to your tasks while a part of you remains in the solitude. You can see your boss as a unique gift to humanity, intended by God to exist in time at this very moment. That realization can help you respond to him differently, especially if he is being difficult at the moment.

Mother Teresa didn't have great spiritual consolations; rather she moved from contemplative mystery to the active moment— by wiping the sick person's brow, feeding the hungry, and caring for the orphan. She saw each person before her as the Christ she contemplated. This perspective allowed the quiet of silent mystery to pour over into her often-chaotic present moment.

You, too, can be unfazed by the surrounding mayhem. It is about tuning in to the voice of God amid the voices of the world. Look at all the people listening to their iPods. Somehow they are able to exercise, clean house, and watch children while in their own little world. Solitude can be found in silence and even in chaos. We need to learn how to rest, even when all around us is frantic.

The beauty of meditating upon the mystery of a spiritual insight amid the mayhem is that it does not ignore the world around us but rather feasts upon silence for a given moment in order to yield a proper perspective for the next step we take during our day. This is the idea behind St. Paul's invitation to pray without ceasing (see 1 Thessalonians 5:17). We allow each moment to become an opportunity for dialogue with God, who longs to speak to us deep within, often through his people all around us.

Whether we are working, driving, playing, or exercising, opportunities to seize a moment for prayer and contemplation abound. With that in mind, what do we actually do during those contemplative moments?

Whatever causes you to consider God is a worthwhile avenue to follow in a moment of silence. Maybe a particular verse from sacred Scripture causes you to rest in the realization of God's love. You might say a few Hail Marys for those you are working with or meditate upon the joyful mysteries. You can pray the Divine Mercy chaplet at 3:00 PM for those entering into eternity that day. Songs or silence, readings or poetry, paintings or children laughing, can all assist you in taking hold of a moment and allowing it to bring you closer to Christ.

For Reflection

1. Do you neglect your need for silence and solitude and allow distractions to dominate your life? Reflect on the importance of silence and solitude amid your daily duties. Do you feel you deserve this time of quiet? Reflect on Jesus' answer to this.

2. What are some practical ways in which you can find solitude daily, even for a few moments?

3. To which avenues of prayer and contemplation are you most drawn?

chapter 13

When the Feeling's Gone: Dryness and Distractions

*P*eople who have journeyed long years with Christ might turn around intermittently to survey the path they have trod. They will find it made up of mountains and valleys. We all long for those mountaintop experiences, where emotion is high, our faith is on fire, and the path before us looks crystal clear. However, the valleys are just as important on this journey, for often deep growth occurs there.

We often assume that these dips in the road indicate that something has gone wrong. After all, we identify spiritual abundance with continual oases, straight and easily identifiable paths, and elevated emotions moving us steadily along. It's true that sin can explain spiritual aridity. Therefore an examination of conscience is a necessary step in discerning the reason for our dryness (see next chapter).

Spirituality is *not* a feeling. Although feelings can be associated with it, spiritual effectiveness does not hinge on warm feelings of consolation. This point is of the utmost significance, in that many people give up on the pursuit of deepening spirituality when the emotional benefits seem to fade.

Many of the saints we read about received dreams, ecstasies, the stigmata, and visions. The common theme appears to be a continued heavenly experience. But these saints sought the Lord, not an experience.

When I was young I was part of a charismatic church that was very open to the gifts of the Holy Spirit. I remember reading a story about a boy who had such a profound encounter with the Holy Spirit that he spoke in tongues for a couple days. I'd read the passages of Scripture about this gift and was certainly open to it if Christ willed to give it to me. People would tell me that he had willed it to all already, so I should simply receive it.

I prayed for the gift in earnest but never had any dramatic experience. Nothing overtook me. It was a very difficult time for me, because it seemed God wished to bless all but me with this wonderful gift. Was I not open enough? Had I not sought him diligently enough? Was there sin in my life that kept this gift at bay?

When I got older I realized that God speaks to each of us in the way that is best for us. We are not all the same. Maybe you speak in tongues and have ecstasies and visions—and that is great!—but my gifts are different. Both of us are called to run to Jesus, with or without the experience of particular gifts.

What does the waxing and waning of feelings have to do with a person's spiritual state? In some ways feelings are simply distractions, but at other times barren roads can be gifts for the benefit of our own souls and the renewal of those around us. I can grow spiritually even if the feelings are distant or not present at all.

St. Ignatius of Loyola is known for having developed "spiritual exercises" that assist people on their faith journey. He highlighted guidelines for discerning spiritual consolation and spiritual desolation. One of his main points is that there may be times when you feel one way, but the authentic path to take is in the opposite direction from that feeling. God created humanity with complex emotions and reasoning, which when used in their proper context bring glory to the Creator. However, multiple problems arise when our emotions rule our will.

If we give in to our emotions, we become their victims rather than their masters. The same thing can be said for the appetites of the flesh, which can cause our bodies to crave one thing or another. We are rational beings, and so we can discern between what we want and what we need—physically, spiritually, and emotionally. This discernment helps us be authentically effective and even happy.

Our tendency in life is to satisfy as many wants as we can. Why? Because we want to!

The average person isn't concerned about satisfying a want over a need; rather the desire is to have all of both. There come times in our lives when the definition of *need* becomes blurred because a certain want assumes a false hierarchy. When we make a practice of fulfilling the wants of the flesh or of our emotions, we begin to see those wants as needs.

As a physical example of this, let's take the problem of overeating. Fueling our bodies with nutrients is a legitimate need; the lines become confused when our bodies begin to want more than they need. There is no deficiency in nutrients that would justify the massive intakes of food that some people enjoy. The disordered demand for food can overtake the will because certain emotions are heightened and long for fulfillment. Rationality is replaced by urgency: The voices of the body overtake the sensibilities of the will.

(By the way, I'm not implying that all heavy people have a problem with overeating.)

With spiritual maturing comes the realization that not every want can be fulfilled, nor should it be. We come to see that there will always be something that tickles our fancy, catches our eye, and seems to be all that we are looking for, but that such a fixation can only end in disappointment. The satisfaction of a want doesn't bring about the joy of a fulfilled need.

This principle can be applied to our spiritual life. Many expressions within Christianity promulgate the notion that true followers of Christ reside in a place of peace, health, and prosperity. However, the fact is that dry periods and trials are part of the journey. Some may attempt to ignore them or "believe them away," while others imagine the barren land to be the actual work of devils from hell hiding behind every rock and tumbleweed.

James says we are to count it all joy when we encounter "various trials" (James 1:2), because something is happening in us, which is likened to refinement. We need to be pure and clean in order to enter into the Holy of Holies, and the dry periods are part of that purification process. We may not feel anything emotionally, but that does not negate the beauty of our continuing transformation.

Another very important area we must discuss—and it is truly practical for our living out the call of sanctity—is distraction. It can look like a thousand different things, but let's use one we are all familiar with, attending Mass.

We get to church, and inevitably a child throws a tantrum because he can't bring his noisiest toy in, slugs his sibling, or soils a diaper. We suddenly wonder if we left the coffeepot on or actually locked the front door as we left the house. As Mass begins we notice that the person in the pew in front of us is wearing a neon-colored dress with body parts emphasized in a manner more fitting for the beach than church. The priest is of course the one whose homilies are the most boring, and we find out that donut Sunday is next week, so the opportunity to bribe the children into silence isn't even available this Lord's Day.

On and on the distractions and difficulties go, and before we know it we are done with Mass. We yell at the crazy drivers in the parking lot, then make our way home to find that the door was locked after all and the coffeepot had shut off automatically, as it does every morning.

This is a time for willing the good in the moment, a practice I discuss more fully in chapter twenty-four. Every moment offers a choice for you to seize: the choice to submit to worry and be distracted or to walk in the grace provided. To will the good in the moment is all you have the grace for, so why worry about the lady with the inappropriate dress when Christ is giving himself entirely to you at Mass? Why worry about your child's needing a diaper, when it is more than likely that three other parents are in the cry room looking to borrow one? In a worst-case scenario you become creative with paper towels, run to the gas station down the road, or head back to the house for one.

You can't live in a place of unrest for too long before going mad. Learn to recognize the many ways you are drawn into distraction and worry, and seize the graces God offers. This is what St. Thérèse of Lisieux did, and it is why she is a doctor of the Church.

For Reflection

1. Look at your journey through life. Name some high mountain-top and some low valley experiences.
2. How have the trials in your life drawn you deeper in your walk with Christ? Were feelings present? Did those feelings bring you through this period, or was it your faith?
3. What can you do when distractions hit?

chapter 14

Sin and Spirituality

As we grow in our walk with Christ and learn to identify our spirituality in the specific context in which we live, feelings will come and go, as will various trials and obstacles, but as long as we are giving our hearts to Christ and doing what we can, growth will continue. However, there is one thing that will retard and potentially destroy the spiritual life in us, and that is sin. Christian tradition insists upon the acknowledgment of sin, because recognition of our brokenness and weakness enables us to see more clearly Christ as our healer.

The First Letter of John says, "If we say we have no sin, we deceive ourselves, and the truth is not in us. If we confess our sins, he is faithful and just, and will forgive our sins and cleanse us from all unrighteousness" (1 John 1:8–9). Jesus gave his life on Calvary to remedy the severe consequences of sin.

The end of my senior year of high school and first semester of college were very difficult for me spiritually. I had one interest in mind, and it wasn't God. Linda and I shared a bit of our journey from promiscuity to purity in the book *Not Ready for Marriage, Not Ready for Sex,* so I won't repeat that here.[1] Suffice it to say that our focus upon one another was such that all else suffered. Family relationships were in the dumps, academics were not a priority, and spirituality wasn't even on the radar.

Our obsessive infatuation with each other demanded a continued catering to self.

As we started college, Linda felt a strong need to change the momentum she was caught in; I, on the other hand, was trapped in my self-absorption—not wanting to change yet unhappy with where I was at. I began to look into some things that had sketchy and even occult-like associations. I focused on my unhappiness, even cutting myself occasionally. I would have liked to foster a spiritual life, yet my past and present seemed to bar me from a God who was so holy and great. After all, I knew the right thing to do and had chosen the wrong instead.

Then God gave me a pretty dramatic wake-up call. I felt him say to me—not audibly but very clearly—that I had the choice to change.

I was invited to a meeting of Christian men at a home near the university. When the evening ended in prayer, I knew that God was asking me to do two things: apologize to my mother for the hurtful things I had done and said to her, and apologize to Linda for the compromising positions I had led us to. My life changed because of that decision to turn away from sin.

Catholics differentiate between mortal and venial sin. Mortal sin is a deathblow to the life of grace within an individual, while venial sin wounds and scars the person's life of grace. Christian spirituality will be destroyed or will flounder depending upon whether the sin is mortal or venial (see *CCC*, #1846–1876). Three criteria qualify a sinful act as mortal: There must be a deliberate consent of the will, the act must be a grave matter, and there must be full knowledge that the act committed is mortal (see *CCC*, #1857–1860).

This makes me think that an actual mortal sin is not as easy to commit as we might imagine. But when someone does commit a mortal sin, the grace or spiritual life within the person dies. The result is a crisis in spiritual progression and expression.

The venial sins we all commit do not destroy grace within us. But they do wound us, and over time they can certainly contribute to our spiritual dry periods.

At Mass we ask forgiveness "for what I have done and what I have failed to do." This is an acknowledgment that our rebellion is expressed not only in our actions but also in a hardening and closing of the heart. If we close a part of our heart to the will of the Father, Satan has free reign in that area. And where Satan reigns, Christ cannot.

As a note of clarification, a genuine dark night of the soul is *not* a result of sin, nor is it the "various trials" James speaks about (James 1:2). The dark night of the soul is a lack of consolation in one's spiritual journey and even a place of complete barrenness. It is not associated with personal sin but rather encourages the individual to cling to Christ via the will and not the emotions.

Sin, on the other hand, is a willing to do that which is contrary to the will of God. It is placing self over God; it is a refusal to love and to be loved. Sin is to know good but to do evil; it is the enactment of pride rather than the expression of love in self-donation.

What keeps us from being truly spiritual is not a lack of feeling but a lack of the will to pursue holiness; it is willing sin over sanctity. When we submit to the demands of a vice, the fruits of spirituality will be limited.

One day I was running through the cemetery, and I happened upon a doe with her two babies. The doe was an experienced mother, and her protective instinct was in high gear.

She seemed to be acutely aware of a possible predator, guiding her fawns away from the awkward middle-aged man huffing and puffing by.

The fawns' nervous energy and their willingness to take flight at a moment's notice reminded me of what our attitude needs to be when it comes to sin. Would that we moved quickly away from possible danger. We need to bound out of harm's way, leap away from potential snares, and be on guard against anything that could destroy those we love.

Instead I think that we, myself included, have a tendency to explore and move toward things that can harm us. Our tendency is to see small choices to be of no real significance. We are not doing anything terribly evil, only making small compromises here and there.

While a person isn't likely to commit murder because of an occasional bout of anger, the practice over time of gratifying self in that way can reach a place we would otherwise have never imagined. A man doesn't wake up one dreary morning and decide that all is hopeless and suicide is the only answer; usually such a tragic conclusion follows a long struggle with depression, belittlements, and insecurity. A marriage doesn't just collapse one evening, nor is it generally the case that a newlywed struggles with infidelity within the first month of marriage. The implosion happens over time.

This is both good and bad. It is good because time allows us to get back on track. It is bad because people can get stuck in habits that seem impossible to change. "It's not how you begin your life but how you end your life." The cliché is very applicable here. We may have made a mess of much of our life, but if we choose to end it walking in the Spirit, then we have followed a glorious path. "Submit to God, resist the Devil, and he will flee from you" (James 4:7).

In his mercy God calls out to sinners, drawing them back to full communion. The impact of sin is so great that we need the tangible healing offered in the sacrament of reconciliation in order to be restored into the life of Christ. Even in situations where a person has committed venial sin, the sacrament of reconciliation is applicable, because this gift from Christ not only forgives sins but also gives graces to avoid them in the future. The more we receive the graces of Christ being poured out through his Church, the more we can be confident about the state of our spirituality.

The sacrament of reconciliation also helps us recognize potential enemies and hazards along our spiritual way. Our vocation in life is to be a saint, so we must be alert to the things that could steal our hearts and stymie our spiritual growth. The *Catechism* recommends frequent confession (see *CCC*, #1458); I like to go at least once a month.

God uses everything in our lives—even our past sins. Perhaps we can assist others in their areas of brokenness. Having frequented the wide road over the narrow at different times in our lives, we can see the pitfalls and know the obstacles others face. Our example and encouragement can be springboards for lasting victory in their lives.

"Therefore, … let us also lay aside every weight and sin which clings so closely, and let us run with perseverance the race that is set before us, looking to Jesus" (Hebrews 12:1–2).

For Reflection

1. When was the last time you went to confession? Is it a priority in your life?

2. Do you feel there is a specific sin that is slowing down your spiritual growth? What avenues toward victory are you pursuing? Would it help to be accountable to someone about this, to share your journey with someone who has permission to ask you how you're doing with it?

3. Is there an area of your life where you habitually place the wants of your flesh over the needs of your spirit?

chapter 15

Virtuous Reality

Virtues are necessary for spiritual victory. Many Catholics are ignorant about what the virtues are; they feel they are abstract concepts that are difficult to assimilate in their daily lives. Although many remember that "patience is a virtue," few realize that there are other virtues worth pursuing. This is unfortunate, because practice of the virtues lead us into deeper intimacy with Christ.

Let's briefly look at the three theological virtues: faith, hope, and love. These virtues are direct gifts from God to us, not based on our ability to put them into practice. How they impact our lives and those around us—their fruits—will depend upon how we understand and apply them.

God grants us these gifts so that we can participate in the divine life! They enable us to truly commune with God. They are supernatural virtues, because only God can provide them; we cannot muster up the ability to walk and live in them on our own. The *Catechism* tells us, "[T]he theological virtues relate directly to God. They dispose Christians to live in a relationship with the Holy Trinity. They have the One and Triune God for their origin, motive, and object" (*CCC*, #1812).

The *Catechism* goes on to describe faith as "the theological virtue by which we believe in God and believe all that he has said and revealed to us, and that Holy Church proposes for our belief, because he is truth itself" (*CCC*, #1814). It is easy to see how this theological virtue is necessary for our spiritual growth. We need faith!

"Hope is the theological virtue by which we desire the kingdom of heaven and eternal life as our happiness, placing our trust in Christ's promises and relying not on our own strength, but on the help of the grace of the Holy Spirit" (*CCC*, #1817). Hope keeps our eyes focused on God when the world, the flesh, and the devil tell us to look elsewhere.

And finally, love is that theological virtue "by which we love God above all things for his own sake, and our neighbor as ourselves for the love of God" (*CCC*, #1822). St. Paul says that charity is preeminent; we must have love in all things (see 1 Corinthians 13:13).

These supernatural virtues are invaluable gifts from God, while we must acquire the moral virtues by our own effort (see *CCC*, #1804). Chief among them are the cardinal virtues: prudence, justice, temperance, and fortitude. These virtues are called *cardinal*, based on the Latin word *cardo* (meaning "hinge"), in that all of the other moral virtues hinge on them.

Prudence "disposes the practical reason to discern, in every circumstance, our true good and to choose the right means for achieving it" (*CCC*, #1835). It enables us to see a clearer path than we may initially notice. It thus enables authentic spirituality. Don't hesitate to call upon God for assistance when you are unsure about what path to take, since he promises to help you grow in this virtue. "Teach me, O LORD, the way of your statutes; and I will keep it to the end" (Psalm 119:33). As with all the moral virtues, the more we practice prudence, the more it will grow in us.

Justice "consists in the firm and constant will to give God and neighbor their due" (*CCC*, #1837). We need to understand the things that are due God and man and get involved in activities that promote those things. When we find ourselves upset because of the way immigrants are treated, women are disrespected, or children are forsaken, the virtue of justice is acting within us. That holy anger will help us advocate for those unable to speak for themselves. An authentic sense of justice prompts us to extend dignity and respect even to people who are difficult to be around.

Fortitude "ensures firmness in difficulties and constancy in the pursuit of the good" (*CCC*, #1837). This is the ability to continue along the right path even when we find it difficult. Bl. Teresa of Calcutta embodied this virtue: She became globally known for her ability to endure difficult circumstances. Only after her death did we learn that she did this for many years without any spiritual consolation.[1]

The final cardinal virtue, temperance, "moderates the attraction of the pleasures of the senses and provides balance in the use of created goods" (*CCC*, #1838). This is probably one of the greatest needs of our time. As this virtue increases in our life, we will find the battle against the world, the flesh, and the devil to be far less problematic. We are made for God, and the things of this world cannot satisfy us. The virtue of temperance will give us strength in reordering our appetites.

The application of the virtues in our life is a guaranteed way to become the people we are created to be. So pray for an increase of virtue, as St. Francis of Assisi prayed before the crucifix in the Church of San Damiano: "Most high, glorious God, enlighten the darkness of my heart. Give me right faith, sure hope, and perfect charity. Fill me with understanding and knowledge that I may fulfill your command."[2]

And thank God for the virtues!

For Reflection

1. What new insights have you gained about the virtues?
2. How can you tap into the virtues of faith, hope, and love, which God has given you?
3. How can you develop the cardinal virtues in your daily life— prudence, justice, fortitude, and temperance?

chapter 16

Warning: Spiritual Elitism

We have all fallen prey to spiritual pride. We have a good week of praying together as a family, and perhaps we begin to look down on the neighbors who may not even pray before meals. Maybe we notice a horrible mother yelling at her sweet child, and we are filled with condescending disapproval, forgetting our own family meltdown a few hours earlier. Pride sneaks up on us.

On the other hand, we have all felt the sting of condemnation and judgment from people who have placed their spiritual elitism out for all to admire and venerate. Maybe your children made some mistakes that became food for the rumor mill, or maybe enrolling them in public school rather than private generated a few uncharitable looks. Or while everyone around you sings the hymn in Latin, you simply mouth the word *watermelon*, hoping no one realizes that you are not spiritually advanced in the language that God apparently truly hears.

Some people seem to equate spirituality with the number of rosaries said, Masses attended, holy cards collected, statues venerated, churches visited, and homeless shelters sponsored. It certainly can be said that persons doing all of those things are placing themselves in the path of abundant graces. But as St. Paul says to the Corinthian church, you can have all sorts of spiritual gifts and even die for the faith, but if you are without love you lack it all (see 1 Corinthians 13:1–3).

Spiritual elitism emphasizes outward activity over inward reality. In Jesus' time the Pharisees were spiritual elites. They looked good on the outside, but their arrogance was harmful to themselves and others.

The idea that our spirituality must conform to anyone else's in action and expression is unrealistic and untrue. This would be an assembly-line spirituality, more mechanical than spiritual and thus not one worthy of imitation. A person praying six rosaries a day with great love doesn't judge the person who can barely find time to pray the one. A person attending daily Mass will not look down on people who are unable to attend; the love of Christ in that person will embrace others in their situations.

What often happens is that intentions are beautiful but the application becomes pharisaical or scrupulous without love. Maybe a person is moved to donate 20 percent of his or her income to the Church because of an encounter with a forceful personality, but after a few months the weight of this financial burden becomes too much to carry. Feelings of failure or spiritual immaturity, or even a realization of having been manipulated, can be overwhelming. It doesn't help if the elitist personality looks at the other as one not as fully committed as previously thought.

This scenario happens in different ways: Look, he isn't praying the breviary like everyone else. See? She wears pants to Mass, so certainly her holiness is in question. Those children can't sing in Latin, and their parents don't attend any of the prayer groups, participate in Knights of Columbus activities, or make substantial donations to the parish.

Spirituality isn't a checklist waiting to be ticked through, nor is it about pleasing anyone but Christ. The cliché that we are before an audience of one is applicable here. We must be careful lest we set up a spirituality of rules, a house of cards that will inevitably come crashing down upon us and others. Let's try loving others as Christ has loved us.

For Reflection

1. Are there any areas where you express spiritual pride? Do you need to reconcile with someone because of that?
2. How have you been hurt by spiritual elitism? Do you need to offer forgiveness to others, even if they've not asked it of you?

chapter 17

A Spiritual Buffet

We humans are physical and spiritual beings. We desire explanations and answers to our deepest questions and long to bring meaningful expression to our internal beliefs. If religion is the human attempt to answer our primordial questions, then spirituality is the practical way in which we go about doing this.[1]

We can see even outside Catholicism the role varying spiritualities have as individuals attempt to answer their inner questions and live life to the full. You may have experienced a variety of spiritual expressions, and perhaps some helped you deal with your daily happenings. We can confidently affirm the true and good we find in other spiritualities, but as Catholics we are also aware of the limitations of certain practices and the dangers they can entail.

For example, Taoism's insistence on living in the moment and not worrying about tomorrow is fully echoed by Christ in the Sermon on the Mount (see Matthew 6:25–34). We can see how things of the past cannot be undone and how worry does not change our future. But it is Christ who brings the peace we are longing for, while the self has limitations that make it unable to realize the satisfaction we strive toward. The Buddha and other religious figures have had insightful words about paths we should travel, but Jesus claims to be that very way we are all looking for (John 14:6). This fullness in Christ does not negate the good found in other spiritualities; rather it completes what is lacking and invites an eternal perspective where often only a temporal one is offered.

Within Catholicism the choices of spiritual expression are diverse and meaningful but sometimes overwhelming. Those looking at such diversity without a clear idea as to what path best suits them can be so confused that they remain neutral. How do I apply all of these saintly teachings to my life if I am not sure whether I am Augustinian, Salesian, Dominican, or Passionist? Which spiritual founder and charism best suit me?

I want to attempt to simplify this ambiguity for you, so that you can settle into the spirituality you can live with.

There is a tendency to place oneself into this or that spiritual camp. St. Paul had to remind people that they were not of Paul, Cephas, or Barnabas, but all are one in Christ (see 1 Corinthians 1:12). Jesus is the unifying factor in all of Catholic spirituality. Benedictine spirituality is not better than Ignatian, nor is St. Thérèse's little way greater than Josemaría Escrivá's *The Way*. The Catholic Church recognizes that each of us has a different vocation and way to live out this faith, and thus the hows of our spiritualities can be richly varied.

Certain saints and their spiritualities resonate strongly with me, while others don't seem to work as well. This is completely OK, because it is Christ to whom we are all united, and our growth in the knowledge of God is of greater concern to Jesus than our own spirituality. Jesus wants you to be a saint even more than you do. Finding out what works best for you is an exciting part of the journey, and it is OK if you change your mind along the way. You can be a third order Carmelite or Franciscan, you can join Opus Dei or a Rosary League, and in the end no one is better than the other; it is a question of what is best for you.

One key note of consideration for me during and after my conversion to Catholicism was this matter of the impact of the saints and their spiritualities. Suddenly I found I had thousands of brothers and sisters in the faith who were cheering me on. The influence of their lives and teachings was very motivating, while at the same time I wasn't sure if I could imitate St. Francis's self-mastery or Padre Pio's intensity. I came to realize that they all had something important to teach me and that I was not meant to simply replicate their lives through mine. Rather I was called to be a unique saint during my own time.

One little spiritual practice that has been very helpful to me is living as if I see the spiritual reality about me. I am not a person given to visions, nor do I have the stigmata or the ability to levitate or bilocate, nor do I possess the charismatic gift of healing. I am just an average guy with an odd sense of humor and a longing to live for God. That being said, the Church, the saints, and Scripture all tell us that there is a spiritual realm where battles are waged, angels are working, and demons are fighting.

I don't see my guardian angel, but I believe this angelic reality is with me always. I don't see Our Lady walking with me, but I often think of her taking my hand and walking me toward her Son. When I go to Mass or confession, I feel her saying to me, "I've brought you here."

I am confident that St. Maximilian Kolbe prays the rosary alongside my family. In my mind I imagine St. Thérèse teaching me her little way, Don Bosco suggesting ways to love young people, St. Thomas Aquinas encouraging me in my studies, and St. Francis and Padre Pio inviting me to deeper discipline. This practice brings great joy to my spirituality.

Why do I bring this practice up? Because I am confident that when we get to heaven, Lord willing, we'll look at our lives and see the constant intervention of the saints, angels, and Our Lady. Then we'll say to ourselves, "I sure wish I had realized how much help I had while walking on earth!" "Look, I wasn't alone in that situation," or, "I sure wish I'd have asked my guardian angel for assistance, since I was never without his active presence in my life."

St. Anthony is far more interested in helping you find a deeper spirituality than in simply locating your car keys. St. Elizabeth Ann Seton is longing to assist you with your kids' schooling, so you may as well ask her for help. The kingdom is a family affair, and the saints in heaven want us to be spiritually alert, for our efforts will impact eternity.

To live in a manner worthy of reality is what we desire. So enjoy the buffet. Take what God gives you; there's plenty for all!

For Reflection

1. Have you felt the pull to join a specific spiritual movement? What about that expression draws you to it?
2. What other spiritual avenues have you pursued and found helpful?
3. Do you feel the impact of the saints throughout your day? How can you imagine them with you?

chapter 18

Sacraments and Sacramentals

We are greatly blessed in the Catholic Church to have seven sacraments and numerous sacramentals. The seven sacraments are not simply symbolic ideas about how God has worked in our past but actual avenues by which we can encounter the grace from God that we so desperately need. Each sacrament brings about that which it symbolizes.

For example, baptism is an actual purifying, cleansing, and new birth into the very life of God. We are born again. The water is pure, and it is a primordial symbol of life. So water with the spoken word brings an individual out of the old and into the new life of Christ.

The Eucharist is the sacrament of sacraments. Christ's body, blood, soul, and divinity are given to all, just as he said in John 6. This encounter with Christ in the most complete way should impact how we live and how we interact with those around us.

Reconciliation is a healing balm to souls wounded by venial sin and resuscitation for those who have destroyed the life of grace in them through mortal sin. The sacrament of holy orders onto-logically changes an individual so that he is forever a priest, deacon, or bishop. The sacrament of marriage is an occasion of grace that enables a man and woman to model the Trinity's love. As St. Paul said, it is a picture of how Christ loves the Church (see Ephesians 5:21–33). This place of complete gift offers grace to assist the spouses toward their final end, the beatific vision.

The sacrament of the anointing of the sick is not simply a symbolic way to offer consolation to someone suffering from illness; rather it is an encounter with Christ's healing grace and a preparation for that eventual encounter with him in the afterlife. And confirmation empowers a person not only to be a spiritual leader in the Church but also to unfold the baptismal promises within time.

Our spirituality must be soaked in the beauty of the sacraments, for these outward signs are true channels of grace. The Church shows us that our bodies are involved in our spirituality, because the sacraments all have an incarnational reality about them. The spirit meets the flesh, the form couples the matter, and we are changed by our participation.

We don't just imagine ourselves being born again; we are actually born again with the waters of baptism. We don't just think about Jesus' gift at the cross; we actually receive him in the Eucharist, and his presence truly changes us into his image and likeness. We are truly forgiven in reconciliation, and Jesus actually speaks to us through the priest, though he may look, smell, act, or speak funny. We are living a spirituality that brings mystery into the moment when we participate in the sacraments. This is the most genuine spirituality, found in the lives of all the saints, because it is actually Christ giving himself to us.

For some reason the importance of the sacraments seems to be minimized in contemporary society. Recently while in Canada, I heard about a diocese that for many years didn't offer individual reconciliation, only general absolution, at the reconciliation gatherings. In the States, too, the decrease in Sunday Mass attendance is mind-boggling. The collapse of marriages is almost expected in our times, while our parishes constantly adjust to the shortage of priests.

There is also a tendency in our times to seek spiritual insights apart from our Catholic roots. I find it amazing to think that the spiritual gems within our faith can be disregarded simply because they appear to be too traditional, exclusive, or enveloped in the trappings of a Church gone awry. Have efforts to find a spirituality outside Catholicism really been better than the proven insights of St. Ignatius and the Little Flower?

Again, we take the good from others but recognize that God has poured himself out to the Church in a very intimate way. The sacraments give grace, whether we feel it or not. Grace is the power source of our spirituality. So being plugged into the sacraments is essential for true spiritual health.

The Catholic Church also finds benefit in numerous occasions of grace called "sacramentals." These are different from the sacraments; they are various reminders of our faith that help us live that faith. Scapulars, rosaries, the Miraculous Medal, and blessings "prepare us to receive grace and dispose us to cooperate with it" (CCC, #1670).

Many of the saints had certain sacramentals that we look upon with even ecclesial gratitude and endorsement, such as St. Faustina's Divine Mercy devotion. The first Sunday after Easter is Divine Mercy Sunday, a day soaked with graces and beautiful opportunities for receiving this mercy. The image of Jesus in the Divine Mercy picture helps us meditate on the abundant love Christ has for us all. Praying the Divine Mercy Chaplet reminds us that we can unite ourselves to the body, blood, soul, and divinity of Christ, even in spiritual communion.

The impact of the Miraculous Medal is almost unfathomable. St. Maximilian Kolbe considered that little medal to be his bullet in waging spiritual war with the enemy.

You may find that for a season one sacramental is more meaningful to you than another. Great! My family regularly prays the family rosary and the Divine Mercy Chaplet, but we've also meditated on the Seven Sorrows of Mary, prayed certain novenas that we were drawn to, and used the prayers of St. Bridget, which focus on the suffering of Christ on the cross. Spirituality is practical in its application, so ask yourself what works for you and your family.

For Reflection

1. How have you experienced the grace of the sacraments?
2. Do you regularly receive these graces?
3. What sacramentals help you in your journey toward Christ?
4. What sacramentals can you add to your spirituality?

chapter 19

Our Spirituality Is Biblical

*I*t is unfortunate that many Catholics feel the sacred Scriptures to be more of a Protestant book. If the truth be told, even though many Catholics can't quote book, chapter, and verse off the tops of their heads, they hear the majority of the Bible in the three-year liturgical cycle if they go to daily Mass. And the Liturgy of the Hours, which is the prayer of the Church—prayed by religious, clergy, and many laypersons—is soaked with Scriptures.

Reading or hearing the Scriptures is essential for holiness today. We Catholics are invited to read them on our own, knowing that the magisterium is there to teach us as we go. The Scriptures are *inspired,* meaning "God-breathed." Many people have likened them to love letters from God to us, and that is a beautiful way to look at them.

I vividly remember sitting on the white sofa next to my mother, in our home in Valley City, North Dakota, and learning my very first Scripture verse, Psalm 27:1: "The LORD is my light and my salvation; / whom shall I fear?" I could only remember the first part of it, but that verse has calmed and consoled me throughout my life.

It is important to read Scripture—but not necessarily from beginning to end. A lot of people try this but lose their momentum in Numbers or Chronicles. I suggest you read the Gospels repeatedly and then jump into the Acts of the Apostles, in order to see how the early Church lived out their love for Christ. The letters of St. Paul can be difficult, but the more you read them, the more key phrases will stand out.

I did read the Bible from cover to cover one summer as a young teen. I remember feeling the intensity of certain books in the beginning of the Bible, the heaviness of the prophets and their messages to the wandering children of Israel, and the powerful statements of Christ in the Gospels. I finished the last sentence of Revelation at my grandparents' cottage in Michigan. But Sacred Scripture is not a book that just came and went; rather it became a part of my life.

Even as an adult I can honestly say that stories I've read over and over again continue to awaken new insights into the beauty of Christ. I often feel like Peter, saying the wrong thing at the wrong time (see Matthew 16:22–23; 26:33–35, 69–75, for example) and yet being loved and used by God nonetheless. Or I look at the boy's loaves and fishes in the feeding of the five thousand (John 6:9) and see my own pathetic gift to Jesus. Would that Jesus would use me to change hearts as he used Paul.

Some people find the Old Testament troublesome, but the Psalms offer us great peace and consolation during difficult times, while the Proverbs grant words of wisdom for our lives. You may be familiar with many of the stories of the Old Testament, but it is always good to read these again and unpack them. What is the context in which they were written? What is going on around the scene? What is God telling us about himself? It is a fun journey, and much can be learned along the way.

There are many books and programs to help you begin reading and studying Scripture, some easier to use than others. One of the most beneficial books for us is the *Catechism of the Catholic Church*, which gives us the teachings of the magisterium, the teaching body of the Church, on a whole host of issues. The *Catechism* doesn't go through the Bible book by book, but you'll find that the two together will be an outstanding duo for your growing spirituality.

How does reading sacred Scripture assist you in developing a spirituality you can live with?

Scripture gives us the truth on our journey to heaven. When we hear and meditate upon the truth, it resonates in our hearts and makes us hunger for God. And sanctity comes to those who are hungry for God.

These sacred words are pillars we can cling to during our difficult moments. They offer us keen insights into why the human condition is so wounded at times. They can give us clarity about what the Lord's heart is in a particular matter. They build within us the very foundation we need to leap into this broken world and do our part to mend it.

Reading the Bible reminds us that we are not alone in our trouble. Like David, we can know that God is the Good Shepherd and the strong tower in our present moment (see Psalms 23; 61:3). We remember that Christ, too, suffered and was ridiculed, and in being like him we also are on a path toward Calvary. The struggles of the early Church can remind us of our Church today, and we can find comfort knowing that Christ will be present to us as he was then.

St. Jerome says, "Ignorance of Scripture is ignorance of Christ." So let's jump into the sacred pages and learn more about our loving Savior.

For Reflection

1. Is Scripture reading part of your everyday routine? If not, how can you make it so?
2. Have you found comfort in reading the Bible? Direction? Motivation?
3. What is your favorite Bible verse? Why?

chapter 20

Mary's Place

*T*he great saints of our faith have always been Marian. Pope St. Pius X went so far as to say, "True devotion to Christ demands true devotion to Mary."[1] St. Bonaventure wrote, "Whosoever bears the stamp of a servant of Mary is already enrolled in the Book of Life."[2] And St. Anselm stated, "God alone is above her; all that is not God is beneath her."[3]

Unfortunately, many people find Marian devotion to be too traditional, boring, or extreme. I suspect they haven't really given it a chance, because I've found the opposite to be true. Devotion to Mary has increased my dedication to Christ and given my Christian walk greater clarity.

Think about the rosary for a moment. We often pray the Hail Marys on autopilot, but the goal is to think about the actual mysteries as we soak in the beauty of the prayer. This dual effort of contemplation and speaking can initially be a little difficult, but over time it takes on a cadence and yields a full-bodied look at the life of Christ through the eyes of his mother.

I would like to look at Mary as virgin, mother, bride, and queen. In doing so I hope to show you a few practical ways that she guides and supports us in our spiritual endeavors.

Mary is a virgin, and her entire purity—body and soul—assists us in knowing how to live in difficult times. The idea of virginity is a little daunting to our modern age. While a few select people have embraced this "odd" discipline, the majority look upon it as something needing expulsion the moment puberty arrives. Why wouldn't a person want to feel good, be with another person in a physical manner, and share intimacy with another?

Both Jesus and Mary were virginal. The Church says that Mary was a virgin before marriage, during the birth of Jesus, and for the remainder of her life. The insistence on this is not an obstinate holding to an unimportant monument of simpler times; rather it is a clear reminder that integrity in body is a witness of that which is to come.

Jesus says that in heaven people will not be given in marriage (see Matthew 22:30). Our hearts will be captivated with God, and the sign of complete gift found in the sacrament of marriage will be fulfilled in the presence of true Love. To live virginity today is to live as we will all live in eternity. Virginity is a physical lifestyle that models our eternal destiny.

Even within the sacrament of marriage, our spirits need to be unstained by the world around us. St. Paul tells the Romans, "Do not be conformed to this world, but be transformed by the renewal of your mind, that you may prove what is the will of God, what is good and acceptable and perfect" (Romans 12:2). Regardless of our vocation, we must all have virginal hearts. Mary's purity of body and soul witnesses to the need humanity has for holiness. The word *holy* means "set apart." Mary was set apart: She is "blessed...among women" (Luke 1:42), and her virginity bears witness to the fact that one cannot outgive God!

Mary is the Mother of God. Out of all time God selected her to be the Mother of the Incarnation of the Second Person of the

Blessed Trinity. The invisible God became visible (see Colossians 1:15) by Mary. The flesh that Jesus received was provided by the body of Our Lady. And the shedding of blood from this very body delivered us from our sins. Mary as the Mother of God changed humanity forever!

Mary is also our mother, and this is an outstanding comfort to us all. The words, "Woman, behold, your son,… Behold, your mother," come from Jesus himself (John 19:26, 27). In the book of Revelation, the dragon goes to wage war with the woman and the rest of her offspring, which is what we are (see Revelation 12).

What does it mean to have Mary as our mother? It can make all the difference in our growing spirituality.

There is nothing like looking at a mother while she gazes at the face of her child. The care and commitment, which start within the womb, are total gift. A mother hears the heartbeat of her child, knows every curve of her child's face, and hears the tiny nuances of her child's speech.

A number of years ago I was doing a youth retreat in O'Lean, New York. (I love this annual gathering of kids from rural areas for worship and encouragement.) During the evening the Blessed Sacrament was exposed for adoration. The lights were dim, and worship music was playing quietly.

I was sitting in the very back of the room, and in front of me a mother began rocking her child in her arms back and forth. She stroked the child's hair, as together they gazed upon Jesus in the Eucharist. I felt as if I were looking at the Blessed Mother lovingly holding each of us. It was a Marian moment for me.

But really, the Marian catechesis was one of the most difficult aspects of Catholicism for me to comprehend. When I moved to Steubenville, Ohio, to finish my master's in theology, a famous mariologist was assigned to be my advisor. I took a few of his classes and was very irritated at his abundant devotion to Mary. It just seemed extreme. I asked myself why was I so upset, and in the end I realized that I was afraid of committing idolatry, giving to a creature what should be given only to God.

The more I read and studied about Mary, the more I realized that the Church taught only what was true. I couldn't love Mary more than Jesus. But I was called to be like him, so surely a devotion to his mother was necessary. I was sure that his love for her was great.

One night I was in my attic, just sitting on a couch, when I uttered, "Mary, I love you." It just kind of came up from inside of me, and the prayer was authentic, if not a little surprising. I realized that, in fact, I did love her. This was exactly where I was at, unnerving though it was. All of the information I had been processing in trying to come to grips with the Church's teachings about Mary went from the head to the heart that night.

I have often thought that Mary comes and straightens my hair, holds my hand, and brings me to Mass every Sunday. I imagine her buttoning my shirt, wiping away a little smudge on my cheek, and bringing me to her Son at reconciliation. In other words, I find that she mothers me, like that mother I witnessed in New York many years ago. I love the fact that she is helping me grow in my spirituality.

Mary knew Christ better than did any other person in this world, and she is committed to knowing us in such a complete way too. Because of her total commitment to Jesus, she longs for her other children to follow his example and to "do whatever he tells you" (John 2:5).

Mary shows us Jesus in a way we would never understand without her aid. She will assist us in loving her Son, always pointing us toward him, and will extend to us the maternity that she poured out upon him. We are truly blessed to sit at her feet and learn how to adore her child.

Mary is a bride. Since she models not only holiness but also maternal compassion as complete gift, she is the standard and guide for us as Church. Mary is the virginal bride, and we as the body of Christ must follow her example in order to be the holy spouse we have been called to be. "Christ loved the Church and gave himself up for her" (Ephesians 5:25). Mary shows us how to give ourselves back to God as a true lover. The complete gift from one to the other is a place of fertility and fruitfulness. The more we are bridal, set aside for only Christ, the more we will impact those around us.

Finally, we see that Mary is our queen. She is likened to the queen mother in the Old Testament, the *gebirah* ("great lady").[4] When Solomon was king over Israel, he placed a throne next to him for Bathsheba, his mother. He "rose to meet her, and bowed down to her" (1 Kings 2:19). Thus he honored her, yet he remained in control of the kingdom (see 1 Kings 2:12–25). Mary, as our queen, continually pours the graces of her Son into our lives. She assists us in our desire to live for the King.

If you simply attempted to be like Mary and depended upon her for your spiritual advancement, I can guarantee that you'd be closer to Christ than you could have ever imagined. Why? Because Mary wants you to follow Christ as she did. She knows that you will be most satisfied, fully alive, and truly filled with joy only when you allow yourself to follow Christ entirely. And she will help you do that.

St. Paul says that Christ is "in you, the hope of glory" (Colossians 1:27)! We are to be virginal, for the Holy of Holies is placed within each of our hearts at the reception of Christ in the Eucharist. We are to be maternal, nurturing Christ within us so we can present him to a world that is still in need of the Savior. We are to be bridal, longing only for Christ.

And when we ask the Queen to show us how to honor the King and best serve his kingdom, we can know that she will help us along the path. This, my friend, will certainly help you be the saint you are called to be. This is a spirituality you can live!

For Reflection

1. Does your spirituality include Mary? If not, is there something holding you back from having a relationship with her?
2. Have you experienced Mary as Mother? If yes, how? If no, can you ask God for a sense of her maternal care?
3. With Mary as your model for virginity, how can you grow in purity within your vocation?

chapter 21

Forgiveness Is Essential

"So if you are offering your gift at the altar, and there remember that your brother has something against you, leave your gift there before the altar and go; first be reconciled to your brother, and then come and offer your gift" (Matthew 5:23–24).

Let's be honest: Repentance and forgiveness are not easy, especially when we have to initiate the process. And that is what Jesus is telling us in this passage: that we must do our best to initiate healing when there is a rift in our relationship with another person. Maybe we're dealing with someone who's self-absorbed and refuses to accept any responsibility. Not the issue. Maybe our attempt at reconciliation is rejected. All we can do is make the effort. (Situations of abuse, of course, fall into a different category and should be discussed with a wise counselor.)

This matter of reconciliation and forgiveness is a matter of the heart. For whom is our heart reserved? If it is for Christ and his will, then we must rid ourselves of the resentment and bitterness that can poison us if we are unwilling to forgive.

What is the impact of holding on to resentment? What is the point of withholding forgiveness? Are we waiting for the other party to admit wrongdoing? If we choose to be generous only with those who are generous to us, how are we different from nonbelievers (see Luke 6:32)? Love seeks reconciliation, and love forgives.

Even science is taking note of the negative effects of withholding forgiveness and the positive effects of granting it. Lower blood pressure, reduced stress, less hostility, lower heart rate, and less depression and anxiety are just a few of the benefits enjoyed by those who choose to forgive.[1] It would seem that when we fail to accept or extend reconciliation, we endure a double whammy: Our spirit is hurt once by the offense, and then our body is undermined by our stored-up hostility. We add insult to injury.

My relationship with my dad was one area where I needed to continually work toward reconciliation and forgiveness. As a young man I struggled with the effects of my parents' divorce. As I grew older and learned some of the reasons for their separation, I felt frustrated and hurt, unable to justify my dad's absence or his unwillingness to be reconciled to my mother. He and I struggled to find common ground, but dialogue often ended in argument.

I was finally able to work toward reconciliation when I came to grips with the choice before me: Either forgive him and move on, or remain in this constant place of tension, embittered with him until he died. Things were not immediately peaceful between us, but each year we found new ways to communicate, to extend charity, and to grow in friendship. The healing in our relationship is far greater than anything I could have gained in a counseling session.

All of us have opportunities to choose healing and forgiveness. It helps to be honest about our own shortcomings. This allows others to put their struggles to rest.

When I was a freshman in college, I had a radical encounter with Christ and felt an overwhelming urge to make restitution for the pain and suffering I'd caused many people. I wrote letters of apology to teachers whose classes I'd cheated in, friends I'd offended, and family members I'd hurt. I decided to burn every bridge to past pain and build opportunities for reconciliation. I received some wonderful letters back from some very surprised people, and I had some beautiful but occasionally difficult conversations. In the end my willingness to acknowledge the ways I had hurt people brought much healing to me and to them.

Even if you've lost touch with people or they have died, you can write a letter extending sincere apologies for the offenses you've committed and assume their forgiveness. For offenses committed against you, write a list and then burn it as an offering to God. Allowing the Lord to take the brokenness and hurt you've held on to will set you free to grow in your spirituality.

Jesus longs for us to be people of continued reconciliation. Even if you have to forgive someone seventy times seven times, do it. Or even if you have to remind yourself that the past hurt is already forgiven, do it. So go, be reconciled to those who have something against you.

For Reflection

1. Consider a broken relationship in your life. What steps can you take toward reconciliation? What would you like to say to the person? Take the situation to God, and ask for his guidance.

2. What does the notion of "continued reconciliation" mean to you? How would an attitude of forgiveness and a willingness to bear the shortcomings of others make a difference in your life? What role should this attitude play in a spirituality you can live with?

chapter 22

Love Means Sacrifice, Service, Mediation, and Advocacy

*L*ove is what we were made for and what we were made to do. True love is the very quality by which the world will comprehend that we are followers of Christ (see John 13:35). Yet I fear that our ability to love is neutered by our willingness to embrace self-gratification over complete self-donation.

I am not sure why, but it is almost expected that our deepest hurts will come from the people who should care about us the most. But do we want to let the actions of another deter us from living in real love? And just because we have been burned by a person proclaiming to be a Christian doesn't negate our responsibility to love.

For many the idea of love is equated with something that pleases the flesh, appeals to the eye, and is the fulfillment of a want. However, true love is not about self-gratification but about complete self-donation. As previously mentioned, the Trinity of Persons pour love from one Person to the others with eternal self-donation.

This complete gift of self is best modeled in time by Christ's offering of himself in the love of the Holy Spirit back to the Father, particularly during his agony, betrayal, scourging, mocking, and crucifixion. The Passion was his total gift to the Father, on our behalf, in the love of the Holy Spirit. It was a redemptive act that we could not accomplish nor ever fully repay.

Jesus willingly sacrificed what he wanted for the will of the Father. "Not my will, but yours be done" (Luke 22:42) should be our cry as well. Real love is not a feeling; rather it is an action. It is sacrifice, service, mediation, and advocacy. We can model these attributes in our growing spirituality.

Sacrifice. Jesus says that we should take up our cross daily and follow him (see Matthew 10:38). While this is a wonderful idea, I am not sure we really think about its ramifications. This is no pep rally: The cross is a place of humiliation and death.

Taking up our cross means doing the Father's will over our own. The more we walk in the Spirit, the less we will gratify the desire of the sinful nature (see Galatians 5:16). In other words, the more we get into the habit of wanting what God wants, the more our desire to sacrifice for another makes sense. The Lord is not looking for forced sacrifice but rather willingness to choose his plan over the status quo. Within a given day we have countless opportunities to sacrifice what we want for the benefit of another; this is truly love in action. We can confidently know that we are expressing love in a manner similar to that of the Blessed Trinity. Such sacrifices can have eternal consequences.

One night I heard a woman talking on a webinar. Her father had been given two months to live. The cancer had taken over his body, and it was time to either get busy trying alternative avenues or say good-bye. An all-natural supplement company, one that I have loved for some time, offered a health option that the father decided to try. One of the things he decided was to stop drinking coffee, and the daughter chose to join him in that. Things were looking up. Some of his hair was growing back, and a dead fingernail was growing for the first time in years.

But it was a long process, at least they hoped it would be a longer process than the diagnosis foretold.

The woman talked about how she and her friends would stop at Starbucks, and everything inside her would long for the coffee she loved so much. But she had made a decision based on her love for her father, and that was motivation for her sacrifice. Every time she was tempted to have a coffee, she thought of her father and prayed for his healing.

This is the intrinsic connection between love and sacrifice that I am talking about. We cannot simply say, "I love you," and think that is authentic. Love demands some outward expression. Sacrifice is an act of love, a gift of self.

Sacrificing for others recognizes the beauty behind the Catholic teaching of redemptive suffering. Our difficulties, trials, and struggles can be offered to Jesus on behalf of those needing assistance. We are all connected in Christ. Our actions impact more than ourselves. We can become a gift for another in a way that was not possible prior to Christ's salvific work.

The Chaplet of Divine Mercy is one way of uniting our sacrifices, brokenness, emptiness, and life as a whole to God via Jesus' self-donation at Calvary. We can also make spiritual communions throughout the day. As we remember our Lord in the Eucharist within tabernacles around the world, we can thank him for all that he has done and unite our gifts and moments of sorrow and celebration to God in the Eucharistic presence. This spiritual communion reminds us of the importance of being intimately connected with the Vine as its branches (see John 15:1–6).

Service. At the conclusion of Jesus' earthly mission, he willingly served his disciples by doing the job a slave would normally do: He washed their feet. Jesus showed that a true leader is one who humbly serves those in his care. This is the man who initiated his public ministry with an act of service at the wedding feast at Cana (see John 2:1–11). The wine Jesus provided there wasn't just any wine: It was the best. And Jesus allowed the family to save face in what could have been an embarrassing mishap.

Jesus made the blind see, the deaf hear, and the dead alive. His ultimate gift of service was to willingly lay down his life for the entire world. His service was a complete gift of self back to the Father in the love of the Holy Spirit. He did it all with the absolute confidence that it was the Father's will.

Our service to our family and to all in our reach shows our love. We may not feel anything, but doing the dishes yet again, offering our time to an individual who drives us a little crazy, and attending to the needs of someone we don't know are ways we actually love.

Mediation. The idea of mediation seems a bit odd when talking about spirituality, but it is absolutely critical when unfolding love within time. We know from 1 Timothy 2:5 that there is one mediator between God and man, and that person is Jesus Christ. His mediation for us has eternal consequences. Jesus willingly lay down his life for us; the impact of sin is countered by the impact of Love. God's generosity remedies humanity's selfish pride.

Jesus is the one who brings tangibly into our lives the reality of God's authentic love. "For God so loved the world that he gave his only-begotten Son, that whoever believes in him should not perish but have eternal life" (John 3:16). God willed our continued existence, not that we would endure in a pathetic state of continued depravity but rather that we would be truly healed, be filled with grace, and walk in the abundance of life. The transition from old to new, loss to abundance, death to life, is the work of the loving mediation of Christ. This is the heart of our renewal.

Christ invites us to be people who know where we have been and where we are heading. We who were previously wrapped in the madness of the world are now filled with the Spirit of God. We who were once trapped in our sins are now liberated from the chains of death. We who were slaves to the flesh and societal expectations have been bought with a price and are no longer our own. We are of him and in him, and all of this is because our sin didn't diminish God's interest in us as his children.

We are called to be like Christ, an entire gift of self back to the Father on behalf of those within our reach. Jesus' mediation doesn't exclude our mediatory efforts; rather it enables our work to be truly salvific. Obviously we are not the sources from which someone transitions from old to new; we are the helping hands and the encouraging words. We mediate to others what we ourselves have experienced and understood. It is a mediation that only we can do, in a specific way and at a specific time. We are the Good Samaritan to those we meet on the road of life.

Mediation is to give to another what we have. I can bring in the garbage cans of my neighbor without his knowing it, and this is service, but if I introduce him to a person he has always respected, I am a mediator. The popular kid at school can mediate his social favor to an outsider simply by sitting next to him. Often the people we serve could do the job themselves, but only the mediator can mediate.

Advocacy. Jesus is our great advocate. The Second Person of the most holy Trinity became a man two thousand years ago and eternally impacted all of human life. The fact that Jesus is truly man and truly God is known as the "hypostatic union." One person, two natures: human and divine. It might seem as if this is not overly important, yet it demonstrates how far God is willing to go in fighting for humanity.

Let's look at the bigger picture. After Adam and Eve willingly chose self will over God's will, humanity became the recipient of original sin. This subjected us to darkness and depravity. It took away grace, God's very life in our souls. The unity between God and man was severed, as was the unity between self and others. The internal peace in which we would have walked was shattered.

Our best efforts in striving for holiness are nothing more than that to which we were called. Loving God, self, and others isn't a way to repay God; it is what we were created for: to be in harmony with the Divine, self, and humanity. Sin expressed in selfishness and pride wrecked this union and harmony.

God did not leave us in this place of disharmony but instead entered time as one like us in all things save sin. In other words, Christ's life gave to God on behalf of mankind that which he was due. Jesus advocated before the Father, in the love of the Holy Spirit, for our deliverance from sin and adoption into the divine life. He fought for us when we were not worthy to be fought for. Whereas Adam shrunk from virtue in remaining silent during the temptation, Jesus fought for his bride, for his brothers and sisters. Love advocates.

One of the greatest examples of an advocate is Queen Esther, a beautiful Jewish woman who was crowned queen of Persia when she married Xerxes, also known as King Ahasuerus. At that time Haman, the king's counselor, wished to destroy the Jewish people; he even had the gallows prepared for Mordecai, Esther's uncle. Esther stepped in, risking her life in the process, to make the king aware of the truth. The result was the deliverance of the Jewish people and the execution of Haman.

Esther foreshadows Mary as mediatrix and advocate. She also presents a wonderful example of how we can advocate for the people in our realm. You may have the opportunity to stand up for someone and save a life, though it may cause you difficulty.

We can advocate for people by praying for them on a regular basis, even though they may never realize we are approaching the King on their behalf. We can advocate for unborn children, for people needing health care, and for the elderly. It might be that the popular kids in school make fun of students who pray in public, read their Bibles, or talk about the importance of chastity, but God is asking you to put your popularity on the line and defend his people.

We all have a Haman in our life: the devil. Satan has the gallows prepared. We who refuse to bow before any but the Lord can be sure that he is ready to destroy our lives. Our God is greater than any foe, but one of the beautiful things about the family of God is that our Lord uses us to touch people's lives in powerful ways. You can be an advocate for a child of God through your willingness to fight and defend.

For Reflection

1. Consider ways you have experienced love from those around you. What did their sacrifices mean to you?
2. How can you love your family and friends better? In what ways can you sacrifice for and serve them?
3. Can you remember a time when someone mediated love to you?
4. How can you be an advocate? For whom do you feel called to fight?

chapter 23

From the Heart

*R*ecently a friend of mine posted this quote on his Facebook page: "God has created us in such a way that everything we do flows from our center—our heart. Make sure that your heart belongs to God."[1]

Strictly from a biological perspective, the heart is paramount to our existence. Without the flow of blood from the beating of our heart, we would not exist. The heart is necessary, but even more than that, it must be vibrant and in good health if we are to live to the full.

When we really want something, we set our hearts on that goal, and everything else revolves around bringing it to fruition. The heart is where the will and the want reside. If your heart is not in something, even something as mundane as your job, it is difficult to give your best. So how is your heart in matters of God? Does your heart beat for him?

What we want is usually what we get. People set their hearts on a new CD, a certain hairstyle, some article of clothing, or even a new car, and that is all they can talk about until it is finally in hand. I can be that way. We all can.

I wonder if every kid at some point in life has wanted a horse. When I was young I would watch *The Lone Ranger* and other cowboy shows, where the men, and occasionally the women, were able to ride with poise from one side of the television to the other. The Indians would ride bareback, seemingly one with their animals. I remember wanting a horse and trying to figure out where I could put it if my mother were to grant my wish.

Expense was always the issue. We didn't have a lot of money, and if we found a few extra dollars, it would be used to buy food, not a horse.

As I got older I had the chance to ride horses on my friend's ranch. They were massive, and to be honest, I was a little afraid when a horse I was riding began to gallop. In the end I realized I would never get a horse. The truth was, I didn't need one. I lived in a small Midwestern town, and my mother had a car that got us from one place to the next.

Through the years I have had many other wants: new cars, sporting equipment, video game systems, and anything else electronic and cool. What I wanted was not always what I needed.

What happens when we don't get what is on our heart? We become depressed, extremely unhappy, or maybe even angry. There can be a deep chasm in our hearts that it seems nothing else can fill.

Here is the secret for your heart: When you fix it on the things of God, you will not be disappointed. The truth is, your heart was made to be set upon him. The more you fall into sync with this reality, the more authentic your life becomes.

When we want the things of God, we will finally be satisfied, because the things of heaven outshine the trinkets of earth. The more we align ourselves with the heart of God, the more our hearts beat in a vibrant way. By placing ourselves in the heart of God, we are able to love our family even in its brokenness, love our friends even if they betray or deny us, and certainly love the neighbors we encounter along the way.

How many times have you wanted to do the right thing but fizzled after a few days? Maybe you were serving the homeless at a soup kitchen or visiting the elderly at an assisted-living facility. Did you give up after a few weeks? The motivation for our social impact must be the heart of God, or our zeal will fade. We must fix our hearts upon the certainty of being in Christ—of having been rescued and befriended and truly in the family of God—and from this reality friendship, familial love, and lasting social service will overflow to the world around us.

Do you want the things of God? Run to the heart of God. Do you find your ability to serve limited and fickle? Run to the consistent love God has for you. His heart beats for you, so let your heart beat for him.

Being in a relationship with God is not simply friendship or family, and it certainly isn't conditional upon whether you feel his presence or have done something to please him. Rather, being in a relationship with God is recognizing that his heart beats for you. This truth will enable your love to overflow to others. We must learn the practicality and realization of being loved first by God in order to authentically love others.

For Reflection

1. Does your heart belong to God? How can you tell?
2. How can knowing God's love assist you in loving your neighbor today?

chapter 24

Willing the Good in the Moment

Spirituality can't live in a world of white puffy clouds and angelic voices. It must be brought down to the day-to-day, even moment-to-moment happenings of life. This chapter will address the "how to" of living your moments as spiritually as possible. I call it "willing the good in the moment," and the starting point for this is prioritizing.

What are your needs—not wants but needs? Consider this carefully. What are the things you will fight for when push comes to shove? Certainly rest, food, shelter, clothing, exercise, intellectual stimulation, and creativity are foundational needs. Knowing your needs will enable you to prioritize the many things that demand your attention. Even though many of our needs are connected, choosing which one should get attention during a day, week, or month can be difficult. This is where the virtue of prudence comes into play.

A need I had to address was getting in shape and staying there. My thinking was, if I begin to exercise, it may take time, but eventually my caloric burn will be greater than my caloric intake. The exercise and loss of weight will certainly contribute to the quality of rest I get, another one of my needs.

I travel a lot, which affects how I exercise. I cannot join a class that meets regularly for aerobics. How could I meet this need in my particular circumstance?

Prioritizing enables us to strategize. I realized that I could change little things one after the other. Over the past several months, I have lost fifty pounds and have almost overcome my insomnia.

Often we exist in survival mode. The many worries and crises that we face demand our attention, and any needs that we would like to address seem to get shuttled to the last place in terms of our daily priorities. We are exhausted, broken, and empty. Our flesh is at its limit, and our spirit is weak. The light at the end of the tunnel is almost out, and the ability to hang on and "do" is long gone. The principles and techniques useful to others don't work for us. We find ourselves despairing that any victory can be ours.

Does that sound like you? If so, that's OK. It is good to be broken, weak, and empty. You cannot live victoriously on your own strength. You will not make it to the abundant life by pulling yourself up by your bootstraps or by numbing yourself with entertainment, drugs, alcohol, temporary relationships, and other self-gratifying practices. You need Jesus, your healer and your strength. You need his peace, his joy, his patience, and the other fruits of the Holy Spirit (see Galatians 5:22).

But how do we get these in our lives when we are so weak? How do we avoid the temptations of the world, the flesh, and the devil? How do we walk in victory? We beg for the grace, and then we *will* the good in *that* moment in which we face the struggle or temptation.

Let's use the weight-loss example again. This battle may be familiar to some of you.

Imagine that I have found a proven diet and exercise routine. I decide that I will commit myself to follow the plan to the letter.

Day 1 is fine, and possibly the second and third days are successful. I may begin to feel great, spending an inordinate amount of time staring at myself in the mirror.

But the fourth day's workout is so intense that I am abnormally sore on day 5. The following day I can barely get out of bed, let alone run or lift weights. The next day I am feeling a little better but am still not able to really work out in a way that will make a difference.

A few days pass, and when I am ready to begin again, the chaos of family life has reached a new high. Time is gone before I know it, and I am unable to do the hour workout scheduled for the day. Maybe I have a fight that night with my spouse, or we go to a late movie, and the following day I just don't feel like working out. Eventually I just stare at the treadmill, and then I begin to hang my jacket on it. The weights collect dust, and my stomach reminds me that this need is still not met.

So what do I do? What can I do? I must will the good in the moment. What does that mean? God does not give me the grace to be victorious once for all without any further struggles; rather he gives me the grace to be victorious in this specific moment when I am facing the difficulty.

Pick the struggle: smoking, lying, fighting, pornography, lack of exercise, overeating, sloth, anxiety, envy, or whatever. Victory will come to you not because you commit to a long-term plan but because when you are tempted, you will in that one moment to not smoke, eat the additional sweet, argue, or gossip or to go for that needed run. It is the thousand little moments of willing the need over the want that will bring the desired victory and habits of holiness.

I hope you're not operating on the assumption that you can

apply another lofty principle to your crazy world and find unencumbered success. I am not able, because of my acute personal weakness and brokenness, to live consistently in victory. I have tried many times and failed. At each crossroads my choosing to will the need over the want is possible because of the graces granted to me by God.

This is why the sacraments are so important. We are able to tap into our baptismal graces at all times. We have received "the special outpouring of the Holy Spirit" through the sacrament of confirmation (*CCC*, #1302). If we are married, we can truly know that the grace is present for us to love one another, even when we don't feel emotional fuzzies for our spouse. We receive the graces we need at Mass and in the sacrament of reconciliation to be victorious in areas we can't achieve on our own strength.

Often we don't feel any different after going to Mass, so how can we choose the need over the want when we still feel exhausted and at our wits' end? The reality of the graces received in the sacraments is not dependent upon our feeling them; furthermore, applying these graces in the specific moment does not necessitate an application of emotion. You can will victory without emotional input.

Here is what I mean: When we are empty, we run to God to fill us up; when we are weak, we cling to the Lord as our strength; and when we are broken, we find our true healing in the arms of Jesus. Even in the natural realm we have some ability to do the right thing; how much more will we as recipients of abundant graces achieve lasting victory.

God wants us to continually depend on him, as Christ did when he walked this earth. He did all things for the will of the Father and as a result changed humanity. Only in Christ will we have victory over our sins and struggles. Only by tapping into God's grace each singular moment will we have the victory to face the next moment with greater confidence. And the more we tap into his grace, the more habits of holiness we will develop.

This principle works in all areas of life, not just coping with difficulties. If Christ satisfies me, gives me rest, and affirms me, then I am truly free to be in the presence of others, to treat them with dignity, and to respect their willing the good in specific moments of their lives. I don't look to them to gain victory over my struggle, but I am free to truly love them—to will love!

Whether you are in crisis control, working against certain vices, or learning to truly love, you need to walk in the moment. To worry about tomorrow or yesterday is a conduit for stress. Jesus tells us that today has enough to keep us busy, without adding the unnecessary troubles of what may or may not come (see Matthew 6:34).

Let it be said that willing the good is certainly the best way to go but not always the easiest. It is particularly difficult if a person has been making habits of vices. Sin can take a foothold to the extent that despair and disbelief seem to rule. The fear of failure can keep people from traveling the road toward healing. They are afraid of not being able to stick to a diet or exercise program, so they don't begin; or they assume they can never be a saint, so they remain in the land of mediocrity.

But the intensity of the struggle points even more to dealing with it in the moment! To worry about whether you will have victory over drinking tomorrow is insane; all you can do is apply the graces God gives for the immediate moment. When you have that desire to smoke, to drink another beer, to say that hurtful word—well, will for just that moment to do push-ups instead, drink a glass of water, or say something kind. It will seem almost impossible, but if you have made that issue a priority, then you will have victory. You *do* have the graces, from prayer and the sacraments, to will the good.

Once you have gained victory in an area, please don't assume that you will be free from its allure in years to come. Don't let pride lead to a fall. You must be vigilant, continually aware that at any moment you could choose wants over needs, numbing self-gratification over loving self-donation. Living this moment and then the next is the narrow path, constantly depending upon the graces of Christ rather than your own blood, sweat, and tears.

While we certainly can develop habits of holiness and experience abundant living in any and all scenarios, the battle against the world, the flesh, and the devil is ours until the very end. St. Paul spoke of running the race up to the last moments of his life, lest he be disqualified (see 1 Corinthians 9:24–27). We may find ourselves dealing with a struggle we thought was conquered years ago or a worry that had found a peaceful resolution at some other point. And the ease of walking victoriously in certain areas will be accompanied by a new set of hurdles. Why? Because as we walk closer to the light, more specs and stains will be revealed.

This is a very good thing, for we are being refined repeatedly as we journey closer to Christ. He will never give up on us. He will go more deeply into our lives and hearts to weed out anything that could take us away from love. That is what we are made for: to love and be loved!

Have you ever thought, "Gosh, I am glad I didn't realize how hard life was going to be, or I would never have chosen this particular path?" Olympians can testify that the total commitment of self to their sport was greater than they could have ever imagined. But whatever difficulties we face, Christ is with us. St. Padre Pio received many marvelous graces from God, but he also faced great opposition from the enemy, even to the point of doing physical battle on a regular basis. Walking in holiness can mean walking slowly and with a limp.

We think of spiritual growth as being up and out, but often spiritual advancement happens deep and within, unseen by those around us. While victory over external vices is applauded and recognized, the deep work Christ is doing—such as addressing pride, insecurity, and mistrust—might manifest itself in some form and fashion that none can fathom.

The person who limps toward Jesus in total weakness has a chance at finishing the race with excellence. The individual who is aware of his inabilities can depend upon the one who is victorious. We are truly "more than conquerors" in Christ Jesus who strengthens us (Romans 8:37).

How do we transition from our emptiness to Christ's fullness? How do we walk in his victory and not stumble in our inability? How do we truly live in a way that is countercultural yet impacts the world that we are part of? We will the good in the moment.

For Reflection

1. Over what habits of sin do you want victory? How can you will virtue over vice?

2. How can you will the good when your feelings are contrary or absent?

3. What sacraments have you received? Do you experience the graces from these sacraments when you need them, even when you don't feel them?

chapter 25

Spirituality of the Senses

*L*et's revisit the important theme of incarnational spirituality. We are living, breathing beings made of flesh, bone, muscles, blood, and other biological material. We certainly have a spirit, but our spirituality is actualized through our bodies.

It is also true that our growth in holiness is not contingent upon our emotions, for our emotions can misguide us. But we do not disengage our emotional tendencies to embrace only the rational in every scenario; rather we allow our will to guide our emotions.

Much of what we experience is due to information that comes to us through our senses. A few of the five senses are more obvious in their contribution toward spiritual awareness, but in fact each one has a role to play.

Taste. Regardless of whether we feel anything that confirms that the Eucharist is really Jesus—Body, Blood, Soul, and Divinity—we do in fact taste his presence in Communion. This is an intimate encounter with God that is profound in its impact on a temporal and eternal level. We are forever changed as we eat the Body of Christ, enabled in time to love with a supernatural love. We are being transformed into Christ's image and likeness, because we are truly receiving his image and likeness. The Lord enters our actual bodies, allowing us to be united to the Trinity.

Touch. When we hold a sick child in our arms, wipe the tears from a young person's cheek, or take the hand of an elderly individual, we are in fact loving as Christ loves. Human touch is absolutely imperative for proper development, true healing, consolation, and guidance.

Jesus was walking amid a throng of people, and a woman with an issue of blood reached out and touched the hem of his garment. The power of touch, accompanied by the woman's faith, moved the heart of God (see Mark 5:24–34). Jesus touched many people in his ministry; he touched the disciples' feet at the Last Supper (John 13:1–17).

Sight. The writer of Hebrews tells us to fix our eyes upon Jesus, "the author and perfecter of our faith" (Hebrews 12:2). The Magi journeyed a long distance to see the newborn King (see Matthew 2:1–11). Zacchaeus climbed a sycamore tree in order to be able to see the worker of miracles passing by (Luke 19:2–4). We use our eyes to read Gospel accounts that enable us to picture Christ and his wondrous deeds and so know him better.

Think about Jesus in the Garden of Gethsemane. Having instituted the Eucharist, he now asks his disciples to watch and pray (see Luke 22:40–46). Being alert, watching, and preparing are associated with Christ's salvific mission.

Smell. The fragrance of a sacrifice offered to God in the Old Testament was either pleasing or not. The fact that Abel's offering was accepted while Cain's was not shows us that God looks at the heart when we lay our offerings before him. What is the fragrance of your offering? What is your heart like as you offer God your prayers?

Hearing. At the liturgy God is present to us in a very real way through the reading of the sacred Scriptures. Many prayers of

David ask God to hear his cry. Do we have a God who speaks, creates, and is a word? Yes! But do we also have a God who hears? Absolutely! This is coupled with the fact that he cares about us, our plight, our sins, our circumstances, and our struggles. God heard the cry of Israel in Egypt (see Exodus 2:23, Acts 7:34); he hears you and cares for you. But you are also asked to hear him when he calls to you.

Oftentimes we feel that our spirituality must overwhelm our senses or go beyond them. We think that God must do something beyond the natural in order to make us truly spiritual beings. The truth, though, is that God speaks to us through our natural senses. Certainly God is not limited to the natural, but because we are body and soul, he will use the senses of taste, touch, sight, smell, and hearing to show himself to us.

Sometimes God works contrary to our natural understanding. Elijah prayed for death as he fled the evil Jezebel, but instead he found a way to live. In prayer he heard a mighty wind, but God was not found there. He then experienced an earthquake followed by a fire, but God was not found in these either. Finally a still small voice revealed the presence of God (see 1 Kings 19:9–12).

There are times when our expectations concerning how God will reveal himself need to be modified. Yes, God speaks to us in supernatural ways, but oftentimes his communication is quiet and normal. Simply put, you are not likely to be the recipient of an angelic vision stating you must go here or speak to a person there; rather Jesus will give you a small, quiet nudge to ask you to reach out to a hurting child or speak a kind word to a person needing to know he is loved. These seemingly ordinary acts can change eternity.

For Reflection

1. Consider the senses. How have you known God's presence in each of these?
2. Have you thought about how God could use you to change people for all of eternity?

chapter 26

Snake Kissing and Other Extremes

I will never forget a cookout in Virginia many years ago with a number of people who had recently attended one of my concerts. We were talking about faith when a lady said that kissing snakes and drinking strychnine may not be too ridiculous in regard to spirituality. After all, they certainly would require a lot of faith.

I was dumbstruck. Was she actually serious?

Good grief, the Scriptures repeatedly tell us to avoid testing God (See Deuteronomy 6:16, Psalm 78:17–22). Christ, during his temptation in the wilderness, rebutted Satan with this (Matthew 4:7; Luke 4:12).

Mark 16:17–18 is the passage that some have used to try and justify intentionally drinking poison and handling vipers. But when Paul was bitten by a snake in Acts 28:3, it was accidental. He wasn't staring into the snake's eyes or handling it in order to prove he was a man of faith. Life is already difficult enough for me without increasing problems by handling snakes. Put it this way: You will encounter enough troubles in a day to keep you busy. These are all God expects you to think about. You don't need snakes to be a saint.

I know what you are thinking: Chris, I don't kiss snakes. Good! But we need to be careful about extreme expressions or demonstrations of our spirituality that can be as obnoxious and ridiculous as snake kissing. By *extreme* I mean any expression that a person embraces along with the belief that this is how all people reach God. It is the attitude that insists there is only one path to sanctity, and that path is mine.

What do these extremes look like? Keep in mind that I am not condemning certain activities, merely noting that a certain attitude behind them can cause imbalance. The problem is the insistence upon any standard as the only way a person can reach God or express true spirituality.

When I was a Protestant, I knew many people who felt that the King James Bible was the only authentic translation for real Christians. "If it was good enough for Paul, it's good enough for me." Possibly you've heard that the Latin Mass is the only legitimate expression of liturgy or that all rock music is of the devil. Maybe you have heard that if you really cared for your children's salvation, you would home school them. Or that anyone who drives a Lexus hasn't experienced Christ.

There is nothing wrong with going to the Latin Mass or home schooling (which we did for many years). Driving a Lexus would be nice; we are open to receiving one if you have an extra! And Jesus will still like you ladies if you choose to wear pants and not dresses. In fact, he will still answer your prayers if you don't go to daily Mass.

The only place where we are called to extremity is in expressing extreme love, extreme faith, extreme hope, extreme service, and ultimately extreme virtue. We must love as though that is all we were made for.

My wife has a saying, "Extremes are easy; balance is difficult." How true. We have found it is more difficult to control the amount of television our children watch than it would be to just call TV evil. But television can be used for good or for evil, and developing a strong sense of right and wrong is key to maturation in spirituality. We need to allow our children to process what they believe and why. Although blisters can hurt the hands, over time they become calluses that protect and allow for greater work to be accomplished.

We can be on the offense or on the defense. If we are on the defense, trying to keep everything outside of our protective bubbles, then we run the risk of embracing an extreme. If we are on the offense, we can guide and protect, ebbing and flowing with scenarios and situations as we come upon them. Everything becomes an opportunity for a teaching moment. Instead of defensively removing Internet access from our homes because there are bad websites, we can implement safeguards and standards. Instead of moving out of town to avoid interacting with negative things, we can teach our children more about how to be in the world but not of it.

I'm not saying that morality is subjective. I'm talking about "gray" areas, not the black-and-white areas our Church insists on.

Going on the offense allows us to train. "Look, kids, here is the Latin Mass being offered; this is how the majority of Christianity celebrated the liturgy for centuries." Or, "See how much love that lady has for Christ as she teaches her children the mysteries of the rosary while wearing pants."

However you attempt to find balance, keep in mind that you will make mistakes. That is OK. You are allowed to change your mind about things, modify your convictions, and flow with the seasons of life. This is a journey, not a standardized test in which you have to get every answer right. Enjoy the moment, but watch out for snakes.

For Reflection

1. In what areas do you find yourself drawn to extremes? How can you bring balance to those areas?

2. Have you felt judged by others because you didn't embrace their convictions? Do you think you've put others in that situation?

chapter 27

Taxicab Spirituality

I have eight kids, and four of them are in sports throughout the year. What that means for my wife and me is many hours going to and from practices and games. We are taxi drivers but without the bad hair. Just the other day I went to the same location six different times to drop a child off for a practice, school, or some variation on that theme. It is realistic to see how this will be the norm for us over the next few years, so I had better find some way to redeem the hours.

One beneficial practice is using those mobile minutes for prayer. If we have a tape or CD player in the car, we can listen to teachings or join in singing some great worship music. Today, on our way home from my son's soccer game, we prayed the Divine Mercy chaplet for a child we know who was in Pittsburgh having surgery.

I suppose this is what life is like for many of you: going from one event to the next, unsure what you'll be doing for dinner, let alone trying to plan a great night of spiritual activities. Some people give up on prayer if they can't get to the hour of adoration or find a quiet half hour in a day. They feel little hope for building any spiritual momentum, and so they give up trying to do anything. But God works in the context of our life.

Although you may not be able to attend Mass today, you certainly can commune with God while doing the thousand errands that await your attention. At any time you can have spiritual communion with Jesus. You can go to the place of solitude deep within even when the noise around you is deafening.

In Fr. Stefano Manelli's classic devotional, *Jesus, Our Eucharistic Love*, he says, "Let us undertake to make many spiritual communions, especially during the busiest moments of the day. Then soon the fire of love will enkindle us." And he quotes St. Leonard of Port Maurice: "If you practice the holy exercise of spiritual communion several times each day, within a month you will see your heart completely changed."[1]

God wants to be with us, and we can be with him! He is present in many ways: A calm pond reminds us of his peace, and the wind blowing through the leaves reminds us of his Spirit. God meets us where we are, not to condemn us but to remind us of how much we are on his mind.

Taxicab spirituality might show up in your crazy life, and not just in the car. It can be prayer for a friend while doing dishes, reading a spiritual book as you pound out the miles on the treadmill, listening to the rosary on your iPod while you walk, or spending ten minutes of your lunch break in spiritual communion, expressing your love for God and adoring him. God has us on his mind at all times; our goal is to find ways to keep him continually on ours. This is real life, and we can enrich it by sending up prayers during our comings and goings throughout the day.

For Reflection

1. What brief moments during the day can you use for prayer and reflection?
2. Choose a spiritual communion prayer to memorize, and use it. Here are a couple options you might enjoy:

My Jesus, I believe that you are present in the most Blessed Sacrament. I love you above all things, and I desire to receive you into my soul. Since I cannot now receive you sacramentally, come at least spiritually into my heart. I embrace you as if you have already come and unite myself wholly to you. Never permit me to be separated from you. Amen.

—St. Alphonsus Liguori[2]

O Jesus, I turn toward the holy tabernacle where you live hidden for love of me. I love you, O my God. I cannot receive you in Holy Communion. Come, nevertheless, and visit me with your grace. Come spiritually into my heart. Purify it. Sanctify it. Render it like unto your own. Amen.

—Fatima Prayer[3]

chapter 28

Facts About Fasting

*I*n my mind there are so many distorted pictures and examples of what fasting is supposed to look like in authentic spirituality that finding the beauty in it is a challenge. Stories of holy men and women living only on the Eucharist, never eating a sweet, or existing only on small bits of bread and water portray things that seem to be way beyond my abilities. I can barely go without meat on Fridays. Besides, fasting is only for Lent, right?

Fasting is not only denying ourselves food and water for a certain length of time: It is denying ourselves something that matters to us for a greater good. Fasting is a spiritual exercise, not a weight-loss program.

Remember my story about the woman who joined her father in abstaining from coffee (see chapter twenty-two)? This was a sacrifice of love for her father, to encourage him and pray for him in his battle against cancer. However, if love is not involved in fasting, spiritual fruit will be lacking.

One purpose of fasting is to strengthen and condition us. Does my body demand that I respond to its every whim and fancy? Do I eat to live or live to eat? If I am constantly satisfying every craving of my flesh, then I am a servant to my body. Fasting can help me reverse this. Here's another instance of willing the good in the particular moment. I can choose to deny myself that soda or that sweet for the good of another.

As with physical exercise, you can start small and increase the intensity of your fasting over time. I don't say, "Here is my New Year's resolution: I will never eat ice cream again." This will likely be broken in a week or two.

Fasting is a discipline. Most of us don't exercise because we are euphoric about the aches and pains, but we do appreciate the benefits of our efforts. Fasting won't always be easy, but the harvest is plentiful.

Fasting needs to be natural. It needs to fit into your life! Some people can fast more than others, and some cannot fast from food at all because of health issues. But fasting can be demonstrated in areas other than food. You can fast from television, candy, golf, or fishing, for example. Fasting doesn't have to be a daily commitment either. Maybe you want to fast once or twice a week.

Be creative with fasting. My wife would say that there are seasons in your life that already demand enough. If you're nine months pregnant and stuck with sleepless nights and overwhelming obligations, fasting from food might not be a good idea. But maybe you can fast from reminding your husband about your circumstances!

The point is that fasting can be done in a variety of ways, but it must all be done with love. We fast not because we have to but to remind ourselves that love sacrifices in time in order to be like Love outside of time.

For Reflection

1. What are your fears when it comes to fasting?
2. What type of fasting makes the most sense for your life?
3. Are there people who might benefit from your fasting?

chapter | **29**

Saintly Examples

*T*he placement of this chapter at the end of the book is deliberate. My hope is that after considering some foundational insights on who you are and where you are, you'll be able to apply spiritual treasures from the saints without blurring the facts about what your vocation in life is to look and be like. In other words, my hope is that the saints' tips will assist you rather than replace your own spiritual journey. And the saints do have some wonderful insights.

Obviously we are all unique, and thus each person's spirituality will be unique in its presence and impact. We might try to be like a particular saint, but that is probably not going to work. Even if we succeed in doing everything that person did, that might not be the path God has for us.

Maybe we think that the saints are so holy (which of course they are) and we're not, so what's the use? Yet our call to be saints is true and real nonetheless. I have a priest friend, Fr. Gordon, who says, "When we want what God wants, it's going to happen." God wants us to be saints, even more than we want it, so let's believe it can happen.

I remember praying, "Lord help me to be a saint," and the Lord said, "Chris, I've given you enough time to do just that." In a panic I thought of all the ways I'd wasted time, and I cried out, "Lord, redeem the time!"

If you are like me, you feel that much of the day can be misdirected and not very saintly. It may be that what we are doing isn't overtly wrong, but it seems so mundane and trivial compared to St. Francis' carrying on his body the wounds of Christ or St. Padre Pio's wrestling with the devil. What if you found out that your daily experiences were the path upon which your sanctity would be revealed? What if saying yes to the will of God in the moment, even in all of your trivial and mundane activities, really carried the weight of a saintly act?

I think it can, because God looks upon our heart, not so much the things we try and do for him. Micah 6:8 talks about what the Lord requires of his people Israel, and it isn't building this or that or denying yourself a million sweets; rather it is "to do justice, and to love kindness, and to walk humbly with your God." This is how we are to interact with God and with those around us. We must give them what they are due, that is, show justice, and also extend mercy. These two things will keep us humble, as we recognize that often God has given us more than we deserve; he's given us the mercy we don't deserve.

So what do the saints teach us? I have a few favorites who have taught me some things.

St. Ignatius was a man of great spiritual sensitivity. As God would have it, he was also a great teacher. He devised his spiritual exercises to remind people of God's love for them and of the fact that we were created to worship and adore God in order to save our souls. Often people are introduced to his teachings via a thirty-day Ignatian retreat. Maybe this is right for you.

God's love begins and ends Ignatius' spiritual exercises. He recommends meditating on the sacred Scriptures in depth, putting ourselves into the stories, for example, so as to reveal our brokenness and our need for God. The result is that we can live for God in a way that honors him and impacts others.

Before his conversion Ignatius was a wealthy and proud young man, and so his spiritual instructions attempt to remedy people's unhealthy attachments to the things of this world. We were made for God, and the things around us should bring us closer to him. If they don't, then they are not worth our time.

St. Ignatius stated fourteen rules of discernment. Now, this might seem a bit meticulous, but his goal was to help us recognize and understand the good and bad feelings (consolation and desolation) we experience so we can achieve victory in areas of our lives where we feel hopeless. He also gave rules for giving alms, for sharing wealth and possessions, and even for fasting. The realization that we can easily get off course is something that he knew and experienced. He once received a vision that made him feel good, but in the end he realized that it wasn't from God.

What have I learned from St. Ignatius? Well, I love the way he invites people to meditate upon Scripture in order to understand Christ better, even if they can't attend a thirty-day retreat. Every one of his exercises deals with understanding and applying our senses to the meditation at hand. St. Ignatius wants us to know Jesus more genuinely, to beg for the grace to truly encounter him in our daily lives. Isn't that what we want to do?

St. Francis of Assisi was another man who struggled with the allure of the world, gratification of self, and various avenues of pride. His father was a merchant, which accorded great influence and wealth. Francis' baptismal name was John, after St. John the Baptist. Certainly the influence of the Baptist would be great, as Francis, too, would confront rulers and all within his reach with the message of repentance, preparing them to encounter Christ.

The young Francis toyed with the idea of being a knight. He was injured and captured in battle, and after a year of recovery in captivity, he felt the need to turn back to God. He eventually determined that he would live a simple existence as a penitent.

In the Church of San Damiano, Francis heard our Lord speak from the crucifix, telling him to "go repair My house, which is falling in ruins."[1] So for two years he repaired churches in the area, St. Mary of the Angels, San Damiano, and St. Peter's. Only with time did he comprehend that his rebuilding of Christ's "house" was to be more spiritual than physical.

Francis was not a mystic from birth; like many today he was a good person who longed for greatness. Unlike many, he realized that God wanted everything from him and not an occasional nod. He left the certainty of financial ease, a worthy career, friends, and conveniences in order to follow Jesus. His self-denial created a stir, both positive and negative. He even stood naked before the bishop to express his renunciation of his father's goods. His continued willing of self-denial and total association with the poverty of Jesus set him on the road to sanctity.

Because of St. Francis' willingness to love, we can speak of St. Bonaventure. The mother of Bonaventure prayed to Francis for the healing of her child. Bonaventure went on to become the provincial for the entire Franciscan order. He also wrote the definitive legend of St. Francis' life, the *Legenda Major*, and he wrote a *Legenda Minor* for liturgical use. Eventually every friary would have copies of these accounts, which were read to the friars annually.

Bonaventure also wrote *The Soul's Journey into God* (or *The Mind's Journey to God*), offering insights into the passion of

Jesus. His writings are comparable to those of St. Ignatius. Both wanted us to meditate upon the life and mission of Christ. "He must increase and we must decrease," as St. John the Baptist said (John 3:30). Bonaventure lived in different circumstances than those in which Francis lived, and he showed us that we can develop true spirituality wherever we are in space and time.

Certain saints had definite spiritual charisms that extend even now to their orders. This is so important to the Church that Vatican II encouraged religious orders to return to the charisms of their founders because they are unique gifts to the Church. We are not all the same in how we live the faith, and that is a very good thing.

In looking at the saints, let's remember that our lives won't necessarily mirror theirs in the practical details. It is not likely that we will walk about without clothes to prove our complete abandonment to the Lord in all things, but we certainly can serve others as Francis did. We can deny ourselves a second sweet and offer a donation to the poor on a regular basis. We probably find ourselves in a milieu that is far from contemplative, but St. Ignatius and St. Bonaventure show us that our hearts can soar when we meditate on Christ's life and passion. Spiritual union with Christ is the goal, and nothing else. In other words, give yourself entirely to Christ right where you are, and know that you can journey toward him in a way that is truly spiritual.

You are called to be the unique saint that God intended for this time and place. You are picked, prepared, and protected to do something miraculous with this gift of life. The Lord understands your limitations and your strengths (his gifts to you!), and he extends his grace so that you can be the saint you are called to be.

So what will St. You look like? Life will not be easy, but you didn't think that it would, did you? Will you choose today to be the saint you are in Christ? I know you don't feel as if you are capable of such greatness, but the God you serve desires your sanctity even more than you do. And the saints in heaven want to help you, because your existence is a blessing to them. You are part of their family!

We become exhausted with worry, distractions, difficulties, and circumstances beyond our control, yet it is these very hurdles that enable us to become the saints we are called to be. God provides the graces within our every scenario and only there. He gives us what we need to take another step, avoid another chasm, bypass another temptation. The more we practice acting upon his graces in the moments we need them, the more common walking in the Spirit will become (see Galatians 5:16).

Bl. Teresa of Calcutta looked at each person as if he or she were Christ. She was asked once if the overwhelming sorrow and poverty didn't bring her to despair or feelings of inadequacy, but her answer was simply that this one in her arms was not going to be abandoned, ignored, or forgotten. In other words, Mother could only do what she could do, and in willing the good for the person in that specific moment, she changed not only India but also the world.

We aren't asked to solve the world's problems but to will the good at every moment. Not only will we find true satisfaction, but we will also impact a world that truly needs rest.

What can you do about world poverty? You can feed that one person who shows up unannounced for Thanksgiving dinner, send funds to organizations that feed the poor, adopt a child through an international program, teach someone how to grow vegetables, or hand out sandwiches to the homeless.

What can you do at this moment to become a saint? Answering this question will allow you to start living more abundantly. Who knows what the end of your story will look like? You can be sure that the one person you will the good for today will never forget your yes.

God radically loves you in a unique way, so seize the moments given to you for his glory. He is pouring out graces and giving you opportunities even now. What will you do?

Rest in Christ, be in Christ, and know that finding satisfaction in him will make all the difference in the world.

For Reflection
1. Do you have a favorite saint? How does he or she inspire you?
2. How is God calling you to love today?

chapter 30

A Spiritual Pep Talk

*T*his is a book about hope. You can do this!

When you look at your journey thus far, I am sure you can think of a number of things you'd like to do differently. That is not a bad thing! Wanting change and trying different practices could better your spiritual journey.

Be careful to avoid extremes. Going full force for Christ is necessary, but you can't pursue full-time ministry at the expense of your family. You cannot follow God in a closer way by ignoring your vocation and responsibilities.

Don't give up either, even if the path before you looks difficult. The victory is already yours, my friend. Remember these three little points as you get ready to head out into the real world: Go! Team! Go!

Go! There is no stagnant spirituality. Continue to run into the open arms of Jesus. That is where your heart longs to be, and that place of joy is where you will be satisfied. Jesus knows your flaws and still longs to be with you. His friendship is unconditional. With the saints, the angels, and God Almighty, you are unstoppable.

It is easy to wander about in the desert, grumbling and complaining. But the victory that you can't see may be just over the next sand dune. That victory is yours in Christ; it is your job to obtain what you have been given, which is everything!

Go! Don't be afraid to step out in faith today and believe for something big.

Go! Don't stop and complain about what has happened or what may happen in the future.

Go! You are at this moment on the path toward real sanctity.

Team! This is not a solo sport. You are not asked to figure out the journey alone. You have a great cloud of witnesses ready to cheer you on (see Hebrews 12:1). The examples of our saintly brothers and sisters should motivate us, not paralyze us. They are here to assist us, not condemn us because we are not like them.

You sports lovers know that the whole team works together for one purpose. When a member of the team becomes bigger than the whole, things unravel. We all have a job to do, a role to play, and it is in doing this as a team that victory is obtained.

You can't be the forward if you are supposed to be the center. You can't be the wide receiver and the quarterback at the same time. God has given you different gifts and talents than he has given me, so why would I complain because I am unable to do what you can?

We are all parts of the body of Christ, a singular unit that is meant to impact our world with love. We are not all healers and prophets; rather the Holy Spirit gives to each person the role that will best suit the body as a whole. Working together as a team, we can love most effectively.

Go! As you press closer to Christ, intimacy with God will allow you to do the job, within the team, that you have been prepared to do. When all members of the body do this, then we can all *go!*

When we move forward as a unit, our witness is authentic, appealing, and life changing.

Go! Do the work that God has commanded you.

A spirituality we can live with is one that impacts us individually but also complements the body to which we belong. It is neither extreme nor complacent; rather it is smack-dab in the middle, a place of holy balance. You are not a spiritual Rambo, a singular hope for a collapsed religion. No! You are a member of Christ himself. The Church is his. You are included in the way, so that others can be brought to the truth and the life (see John 14:6).

A spirituality you can live with brings life to others. The time is right, the moment is now! You can do this!

For Reflection

1. How many of these books will you buy for your friends?
2. What unique gift do you bring to the body of Christ?
3. How do you see yourself as a team player? What members of the team are close to you? How do you tap into their skills to help you achieve victory?
4. What are you waiting for? Go!

Chapter Two: It's All About Relationship

1. See Pope Paul VI, *Nostra Aetate*, Declaration on the Relation of the Church to Non-Christian Religions, October 28, 1964, www.vatican.va, 1.
2. See *Nostra Aetate,* 2.
3. C.S. Lewis, *Mere Christianity* (New York: Simon & Schuster, 1996), p. 56.

Chapter Four: Weakness Needs a Helping Hand

1. Liturgy of the Hours, verse and response at the beginning of prayer, adapted from Psalms 38:22; 141:1.

Chapter Five: Emptied to Be Filled

1. Thomas Merton, *Thoughts in Solitude* (New York: Farrar, Strauss, and Giroux, 1958), p. 79.

Chapter Eleven: God Chooses You!

1. See Matthew Kelly, *The Rhythm of Life: Living Every Day with Passion & Purpose* (New York: Fireside, 2005).
2. Teresa of Avila, as quoted at www.thecatholicspirit.com.

Chapter Fourteen: Sin and Spirituality

1. See Chris and Linda Padgett, *Not Ready for Marriage, Not Ready for Sex: One Couple's Return to Chastity* (Cincinnati: Servant, 2006).

Chapter Fifteen: Virtuous Reality

1. See the collection of Blessed Teresa's letters, *Mother Teresa: Come Be My Light.* Brian Kolodiejchuk, ed. (New York: Image, 2009).
2. www.americancatholic.org.

Chapter Seventeen: A Spiritual Buffet

1. See *Nostra Aetate,* 1.

Chapter Twenty: Mary's Place

1. Pope Pius X, as quoted in Francis Edward Nugent, *Fairest Star of All* (Patterson, N.J.: St. Anthony Guild, 1956), p. 1.
2. Bonaventure, as quoted in Nugent, p. 23.
3. Anselm, as quoted in Nugent, p. 17.

4. Scott Hahn, *Hail, Holy Queen: The Mother of God in the Word of God* (New York: Doubleday, 2001), p. 79. See chapter 4, "Power Behind the Throne," for more on Mary's queenship.

Chapter Twenty-One: Forgiveness Is Essential

1. See Katherine M. Piderman, "Forgiveness: Letting Go of Grudges and Bitterness," December 8, 2007, www.mayoclinic.com.

Chapter Twenty-Three: From the Heart

1. Howard Thurman, as quoted in Paul Wesley Chilcote, *Changed from Glory into Glory—Wesleyan Prayers for Transformation* (Nashville: Upper Room, 2005), p. 11.

Chapter Twenty-Seven: Taxicab Spirituality

1. Stefano M. Manelli, *Jesus, Our Eucharistic Love: Eucharistic Life Exemplified by the Saints* (New Bedford, Mass.: Franciscan Friars of the Immaculate, 1996), p. 65.

2. www.ourcatholicprayers.com.

3. www.ourcatholicprayers.com.

Chapter Twenty-Nine: Saintly Examples

1. Omer Englebert, *St. Francis of Assisi: A Biography* (Ann Arbor, Mich.: Servant, 1979), p. 33.

ABOUT THE AUTHOR

Chris Padgett is an author, singer, songwriter, and international speaker. He has a master's degree in theology from Franciscan University of Steubenville and is completing his doctoral degree with an emphasis in Marian studies from the International Marian Research Institute in Dayton, Ohio. Chris and his wife, Linda, are the authors of *Not Ready for Marriage, Not Ready for Sex: One Couple's Return to Chastity*. They are the parents of eight children and live in Steubenville, Ohio. You can find out more at www.chrispadgett.org.